THE 7 INDISPUTABLE LAWS OF FINANCIAL LEADERSHIP

RODNEY BALLANCE, JR.

"THE FATHER OF FINANCIAL LITERACY"
— Zig Ziglar's longtime publicist Wally Cato

THE 7 INDISPUTABLE LAWS OF FINANCIAL LEADERSHIP

AMBASSADOR INTERNATIONAL
GREENVILLE, SOUTH CAROLINA & BELFAST, NORTHERN IRELAND

www.ambassador-international.com

The 7 Indisputable Laws of Financial Leadership
Why Money Management is a Thing of the Past

Printed in the United States of America

ISBN: 978-1-62020-217-3
eISBN: 978-1-62020-316-3

Author photo: Bill Goode / Bill Goode Photography
Cover design: Hannah Stanley
Typesetting: Matthew Mulder
E-book conversion: Anna Riebe

AMBASSADOR INTERNATIONAL
Emerald House
427 Wade Hampton Blvd.
Greenville, SC 29609, USA
www.ambassador-international.com

AMBASSADOR BOOKS
The Mount
2 Woodstock Link
Belfast, BT6 8DD, Northern Ireland, UK
www.ambassadormedia.co.uk

The colophon is a trademark of Ambassador

DEDICATION

I'm dedicating this book to my amazing and beautiful wife Heather. Your patience, understanding, and constant encouragement over the years have enabled me to achieve goals of which once I could only dream.

Thank you for always being there for me, especially through the rough times.

CONTENTS

INTRODUCTION

IF YOU'VE BEEN LOOKING FOR a "tell all" book from someone who's been on the inside, revealing the secrets that companies spend billions of dollars every year to keep you from knowing, this is it. Strap yourself in, because it's about to be a bumpy and unsettling ride for some of you.

In this book, you will learn how you have been taken advantage of by a system that exists for the sole purpose of separating you from your money. This system has been so successful (for those who created it) that you don't even know you're being used, or how.

The companies and individuals who implement these strategies—which you are about to learn—continue to get stronger and wealthier, the longer they can keep you in the dark. The longer they can manipulate your financial moves, the wealthier they can become by using the very money you work so hard to earn.

But the time for keeping us enslaved to their ways is over. The time to take action is now! The information you need is in this book. The actions you need to take are spelled out clearly and in an easy-to-understand manner.

The help that you need to make this change happen is already in place, just waiting for you to decide that you want to stop being the slave and start being the master of your financial future.

THE MASTER AND THE SLAVE

YOU ARE ABOUT TO BE introduced to one of the most vile and perverted industries in the world today. The things I've seen and experienced in this business are absolutely disgusting.

It's time I blow the whistle and expose this business for what it is. I'll also share what we must do if we are ever to stop being enslaved and start being the masters of our own future.

For several decades, I was right in the middle of this mess. I earned a very good living by doing exactly as I was told, in order to keep my job.

I was finally forced to make a decision between providing for my family by being part of the lie, or giving up all the personal benefits but revealing the truth to protect the public. I decided to share my inside knowledge with you, and let you decide how to use it.

At first glance, you might think I'm describing a criminal enterprise, like human trafficking. But no, even though components from this disgusting practice are indeed present, I'm talking about a very much in-the-open industry that advertises itself on television, radio, and in print. I'm talking about an industry that is so much a part of our everyday lives that we take it for granted, and are victimized without even knowing it.

11

I'm talking about the financial services industry. I'm talking about banks, investment firms, and insurance companies. If you thought you knew about the financial industry, hold on to your shorts, because you're about to learn more than you might even want to know.

After reading this book you will have no doubt that banks, investment firms, and insurance companies exist for one reason, and one reason alone: to separate you from your hard-earned cash. After all, the only person who can benefit from your money is the one who actually has access to it—and these companies most definitely intend to benefit.

These companies work very hard and are quite successful at causing you to freely give them your money, so they can profit from access to it. They use catchy slogans, slick sales gimmicks, and pay spokespeople millions of dollars to trick you into falling for their messages.

Equally important is the role governments around the world play in this matter, as they endorse and perpetuate an industry that is nothing more than a wolf in sheep's clothing. The financial services industry has turned governments into pawns in their scheme to control our every purchase and financial move.

Let me first clarify that I am not an economist. I understand economics and how to use economic principles to multiply assets, but I do not have a doctorate in economics. I believe that by being a regular person just like you, my readers, and not some cerebral elitist, I bring a unique perspective to this issue that is vitally needed today.

One economic fact you do need to know is this: just as in physics, for every economic action there is also an opposite and equal reaction.

For example, historically speaking, every time any nation enacts a round of *quantitative easing* (the printing of additional currency), that nation experiences a round of inflation within 24 months from that action.

Unfortunately, each time a round of quantitative easing occurs, the resulting inflation just piles on top of the inflation from the last round of printing money. This compounds the inflation problem, thereby making it more and more difficult for people to afford the necessities of life.

The perfect modern-day example of this problem is the country of Zimbabwe: their inflation destroyed their currency and ripped apart their country. I'll refer to a piece titled "R.I.P. Zimbabwe Dollar," written by Steve H. Hanke, Professor of Applied Economics at The Johns Hopkins University and Senior Fellow at The Cato Institute. Professor Hanke does a fantastic job of documenting the cause and effect of what caused the hyperinflation and the eventual demise of the Zimbabwe dollar.

Other authors have attributed the economic collapse of Zimbabwe to the loss of property rights and other failed stimulus incentives, but the bottom line is the country printed so much money that they flooded the market. The glut of currency reduced people's demand for it, thereby reducing their dollar's buying power by over 12,000%.

The action is printing more money in an effort to provide financial liquidity, and the reaction is higher prices for the consumer, on everything from groceries to gasoline. When policymakers, controlled by big banks, inject more currency into the system, they actually reduce the buying power of that currency.

Action: Print more money. **Reaction:** Reduced value of that money.

To bring it down to your family's personal financial situation, let's look at it this way. If you found a rare collectible baseball card in your grandparents' attic that was valued at $10,000, you would rejoice and imagine all the great things you would do with that money, right? The value of the card is so high because (let's say) there are only 3 of these cards still remaining in circulation, or available to the public.

Now let's assume that at the very moment you found your card, someone else uncovered a cache of the very same card. They found 30,000 cards in a box at the factory which originally made the cards, and all of them were in mint condition. Collectors would no longer desire your card, because now they could get one almost anywhere. Now your card is only worth, say, $1 instead of $10,000, because it's no longer a rare item; the card has become devalued because there are now so many of them.

In a similar fashion, the stock market rallies when more money is introduced into the financial system, because the stockbrokers suddenly have more money to play with. The US Federal Reserve and other central banks flood the system with more money in an effort to provide an economic stimulus for their country. Unfortunately, what they are also doing is providing a vehicle by which the rich can get richer on the backs of retired people and the hard-working folks just like you, who are trying to provide for their families.

You see, for generations, retirees have relied on high interest rates to offer them a safe and predictable income from their savings accounts, and they have relied on their savings to supplement their Social Security or other pension income. So when a central bank forces interest rates lower—to encourage people to borrow more money instead of saving it—they are also punishing the people who are trying to save money safely.

Action: Lower interest rates. **Reaction(s):** Punish savers and promote indebtedness.

The only people this philosophy helps are those who make money by lending to others. When people cannot afford to buy the things they need, they have to borrow money from someone else. Since the world economy now operates on the *debt standard*, and not the *gold standard*, those who profit from lending are of course the banks—who are at the forefront of making the financial rules.

Can you see the genius behind this type of financial system? Financial institutions create an environment in which the only way people can afford to buy what they need is to borrow from the ones who created the financial problems in the first place.

FINANCIAL LEADERSHIP

When someone initiates change, they usually intend to benefit from that change. When we talk about financial or economic change, we refer to what I call *Financial Leadership*. No one can benefit from the use of your money until they figure out how to get you to allow them to use your money, or they simply cause you to give them that money.

While the borrowers and financial slaves to this system practice *Money Management*, those who make the rules and profit from the desperation and despair of others also create the very changes to which their financial slaves must react. These rule-makers—the banks and lending companies—are not practicing Money Management, they are practicing *Financial Leadership*. (I will explain this phrase in greater detail in the next section.)

Action: Drive prices higher. **Reaction:** People must borrow to keep pace with increasing prices.

Listen to what some prominent thinkers and statesmen had to say about these issues.

If the American people ever allow private banks to control the issue of their currency, first by inflation, then by deflation, the banks... will deprive the people of all property until their children wake-up homeless on the continent their fathers conquered...The issuing power should be taken from the banks and restored to the people, to whom it properly belongs. (**Thomas Jefferson,** in the debate over the *Re-charter of the Bank Bill*, 1809)

It's not only America's founding fathers who recognized this threat hundreds of years ago. Listen to what a founder of one of the most economically sound countries on Earth had to say in the 1800s.

The death of Lincoln was a disaster for Christendom. There was no man in the United States great enough to wear his boots and the bankers went anew to grab the riches. I fear that foreign bankers with their craftiness and tortuous tricks will entirely control the exuberant riches of America and use it to systematically corrupt civilization. (**German Chancellor Otto von Bismarck** [1815-1898], after the Lincoln assassination)

But let's not just hear from government officials. What did one of the most iconic figures in the history of business have to say about the banking industry?

It is well enough that people of the nation do not understand our banking and money system, for if they did, I believe there would be a revolution before tomorrow morning. (**Henry Ford**, founder of the Ford Motor Company)

What Mr. Ford said is exactly what I am encouraging the working class people of the world to do: *stage a peaceful economic revolution.* It is not only what needs to be done, it is what must be done if we are ever to escape the economic slave masters who currently manipulate and control the entire financial world.

My last quote is from our American Declaration of Independence, but it relates to all mankind.

> *When in the Course of human events, it becomes necessary for one people to dissolve the political bands which have connected them with another, and to assume among the powers of the earth, the separate and equal station to which the Laws of Nature and of Nature's God entitle them, a decent respect to the opinions of mankind requires that they should declare the causes which impel them to the separation.*

> *We hold these truths to be self-evident, that all men are created equal, that they are endowed by their Creator with certain unalienable Rights, that among these are Life, Liberty and the pursuit of Happiness.--That to secure these rights, Governments are instituted among Men, deriving their just powers from the consent of the governed, --That whenever any Form of Government becomes destructive of these ends, it is the Right of the People to alter or to abolish it, and to institute new Government…*

> *When a long train of abuses and usurpations, pursuing invariably the same Object evinces a design to reduce them under absolute Despotism, it is their right, it is their duty, to throw off such Government, and to provide new Guards for their future security.*

What I am recommending is that every hard-working person in the world today take a close look at where each of their dollars, euros, pounds, etc… is going. You need to ask yourself: "Who is my money working for?" If you are profiting from the use of your money more than someone else, you are probably making good decisions, and are likely practicing Financial Leadership.

If, on the other hand, you are simply reacting to economic challenges, and someone else is going to use your money to benefit themselves more than you, then you are merely practicing Money Management, and you need to create an action for your money that will cause a different reaction. You need to cause your money to work harder for yourself than for someone else.

I cannot stress too strongly the importance of making the change to practicing Financial Leadership immediately! The longer you wait to implement proactive financial strategies, the greater the likelihood of personal economic catastrophe.

And not only economic catastrophe for you, but possibly even for the global economy. Let me explain.

It's been said that when America gets the sniffles, the rest of the world gets the flu. That's because America, now the 2nd largest economy on Earth behind the European Union, has been the economic engine powering the financial stability that the world has enjoyed since the 1950s.

So when Americans cannot afford to import goods from other countries, we create a serious negative impact on those countries, because their economies depend on our economic strength. And just as with the physical flu, if the sick person is already malnourished or weak or has other diseases, and they are left untreated, they can become extremely sick indeed (as happened in the Great Depression, for example.)

Action: Americans can't buy foreign goods because of inflation. **Reaction:** Foreign economies get sick, and the conditions for global economic catastrophe are created.

To understand the timeline that exists for the potential destruction of America's economy, I want to share with you a document from the last century. "The Cycle of Nations" was written by the American free-market advocate Henning Webb Prentis Jr.,[1] who observed the economic paths that the major nations of the world have followed down through human history.

As a student of history and one who was also intimately familiar with our modern economic conditions, Prentis warned us in 1943 of a clear and present danger to our way of life and our economic well-being.

As you read this profound and prophetic warning, try to pinpoint where your country is in this cycle.

THE CYCLE OF NATIONS:
1. From bondage to spiritual faith
2. From spiritual faith to great courage
3. From courage to liberty
4. From liberty to abundance
5. From abundance to selfishness
6. From selfishness to complacency
7. From complacency to apathy
8. From apathy to fear
9. From fear to dependency
10. From dependency back again into bondage

---

1   Loren Collins, "The Truth About Tytler", found at www.lorencollins.net/ tytler.html

Action: America becomes a third world country. **Reaction:** Americans become financial slaves to the rest of the world.

IT'S NOT YOUR FAULT: YOU'RE THE VICTIM!

FROM A PERSONAL PERSPECTIVE, YOU start becoming a victim when you tell marketing companies exactly how they need to design their plans to gain access to even more of your hard-earned money.

Later in this book I'll give you some examples of flat-out lies that for decades have been sold to the public as facts, and who benefits from these lies.

I promise to offer solutions for you though, not just spotlight the problems. Much like seeing that first roach in your kitchen as you turn on the light in the middle of the night, I want to shine a bright light on the financial world and watch the insects in fancy suits scurry for cover. Once we realize we have an infestation, we typically act decisively to recover our property from the swarm of filth. The knowledge I'll share with you in this book will cause you to be angered and empowered to take back control over the money you work so hard to earn.

As I said in the previous section, we must start a (peaceful) revolution to recover the power of our money from those who wish to control us with it. Only then can we begin using our money to accomplish the things in life we truly want to do. Throughout history, when they became fed up with being taken advantage of, people have risen up and revolted against those who enslaved them.

Those are very strong words, I know. How can I say that we've been enslaved, you might ask? To fully grasp what I'm talking about, we first need to understand the word *marketing*. Marketing is different from public relations, which is different from advertising. If you were asked how companies try to control your spending habits, your first thought would likely be: through their advertising efforts. Advertising is one aspect of how they control us, but advertising starts with marketing research.

MINING YOUR DATA

Companies spend hundreds of millions of dollars each year to learn what you are buying and why. Companies such as Visa and MasterCard collect data based on each purchase you make, and then sell this data to marketing companies and retailers so they can design attractive ways to persuade you to give them more of your money.

Here's a direct quote from a New York Times article written by Charles Duhigg and published on February 16, 2012, that's a perfect example of what I'm telling you. Mr. Duhigg interviewed Andrew Pole, a marketing expert for the Target Corporation. Discussing buying habits of Target customers, Mr. Pole commented, "If you use a credit card or a coupon, or fill out a survey, or mail in a refund, or call the customer help line, or open an e-mail we've sent you or visit our Web site, we'll record it and link it to your Guest ID...**We want to know everything we can.**" [bolding mine]

The Times article continues: "Also linked to your Guest ID is demographic information like your age, whether you are married and have kids, which part of town you live in, how long it takes you to drive to the store, your estimated salary, whether you've moved recently, what credit cards you carry in your wallet and what Web sites you visit.

"Target can buy data about your ethnicity, job history, the magazines you read, if you've ever declared bankruptcy or got divorced, the year you bought (or lost) your house, where you went to college, what kinds of topics you talk about online, whether you prefer certain brands of coffee, paper towels, cereal or applesauce, your political leanings, reading habits, charitable giving and the number of cars you own."

The industry term used to describe the gathering of your personal information is as revealing as the act itself. Because this information is more valuable than gold to the companies collecting and using it, they refer to the process of obtaining our buying habits and personal information as "mining."

Target isn't the only company "mining" your personal information. Even the United States Postal Service uses this personal data, to find out how to cause us to buy what they have to offer.

In fact, there's an entire industry built around analyzing your every move: it's called *predictive analytics*. There is even a conference, Predictive Analytics World. There is also a predictive analytics conference for government entities, so governments can know what we are planning to do before we do it, and so better control us. You can learn more about this industry and their conferences at their website, www.predictiveanalyticsworld.com.

Here are some agenda excerpts from the 2012 Predictive Analytics World in San Francisco held on April 14-19, 2012. These excerpts demonstrate the depth of information being mined from us every day, and how companies use it not just to predict what we will buy, but also to implement strategies to control our habits.

- Thought Leadership Case Study: *CA General Underwriters Insurance:* "Seize the Competitive Future through a Shared Vision for Value Creation, Quality Management & Collaboration"

Predictive Analytics facilitates "anticipating future needs so we can actively create the future" (Drucker). Enrich it and your organization by creating more value from predictions, managing prediction quality and genuine collaboration among stakeholder teams. Stakeholders include your prediction financers, owners and users plus analytics developers, implementers and insurers. Explore "what to do and how to do it" for collaboration, quality management and value creation plus appreciate Drucker's Philosophies, Deming's Principles, Juran's Processes and Ackoff's Pitfalls. Tribal cultures and their immune systems are primary inhibitors of collaboration. To ensure competitive future success of Predictive Analytics, we need to selectively relax them.

- Sponsored Lab Session: Live Topical Demo: "Heterogeneous Social Media Analysis: Network Analytics meets Text Mining with KNIME"

Text mining social media data is slowly gaining in relevance and ease of use. At the same time, network analytic techniques are emerging that provide new analytic perspectives to social media data.

This paper shows how combining text mining and network mining can reveal new heterogeneous insights into customer behavior in social media that were not detectable using either technique alone. Sentiment analysis from online forum posts together with reference structures from the quotation network allows not only the detection of negative or positive influencers but the relative weighting of those influencers in the underlying discussion forum.

Originally performed for a major European telco, the techniques and methods presented here use publicly available data and the KNIME open source data mining platform to demonstrate the procedures and benefits of the analysis approach for social media. A conclusion is drawn about the relevance and practicalities of this new approach along with a recommendation for next steps.

- Forecasting Case Study: *Wells Fargo Securities:* "Macroeconomic Forecasting, Consensus & Individual Forecaster: A Real-Time Approach"

This study provides a real-time short-term macroeconomic forecasting approach that offers several advantages over conventional short-term forecasting procedures. The approach produces more accurate real-time forecasts compared to those of the Bloomberg real-time consensus forecast, on average, for major macroeconomic variables. This study sheds light on five important areas of macroeconomic forecasting.

- Special Plenary Session - Case Studies: *Anheuser-Busch, Dept. Homeland Security, & US Postal Service Office of Inspector General:* "Becoming an Ace with a Robot as your Wingman"

Humans and computers have strengths that are more complementary than alike – to the point where a sophisticated algorithm may be the best "2nd person" to put on a complex task. By contrasting natural and artificial intelligence we will explore how to optimize the man/machine partnership.

You can imagine how expensive obtaining all this information is, and also the importance to these companies of keeping how and why they obtain it "top secret."

In the financial services industry, the department charged with protecting this vital knowledge is called the compliance department. Every bank, investment firm, and insurance company in operation today has a compliance department, and this department has the final word in whether or not a representative of that company can say any particular word, phrase, sentence—or even think a particular thought.

Before a company representative can make any statement that hasn't been scripted for them, they must have it approved by the compliance department. The compliance department must approve every company brochure designed to sell products, and they even monitor employee e-mails to make sure employees aren't trying to leak corporate secrets.

Every employee knows that they must never cross the compliance department, or even question their authority. Although they are only small parts of very large companies, compliance departments are the most powerful people in the multi-billion dollar financial services business: you play ball the way they tell you to, or you don't play.

Financial companies often refer to this department as the "consumer protection" area of the operation, but in reality, this department is where censorship runs amok. If the public had any idea what goes on behind their closed-door training sessions and strategy meetings, these companies would stand to lose hundreds of billions of dollars.

This is one reason why banks, investment firms, and insurance companies retain strict control over every word their people say to anyone. These companies know that if the public knew what they are actually doing, their world would be turned upside down before the sun rose the next morning.

As Henry Ford said, *"It is well enough that people of the nation do not understand our banking and monetary system, for if they did, I believe there would be a revolution before tomorrow morning."* This is from a man who was president of a bank in Dearborn, Michigan. Mr. Ford despised the banking industry, and especially Wall Street investment banks, because of what they had done to working-class Americans.

An even earlier warning about our banking industry came from a former President of the United States of America. Thomas Jefferson said, *"I believe that banking institutions are more dangerous to our liberties than standing armies."*

With warnings from men like Ford and Jefferson, why haven't the American people listened and taken control over their money? Why have we allowed ourselves to become a country of debtors? Why do we continue to allow ourselves to fall deeper and deeper into the trap laid before us over hundreds of years?

Nathaniel Rothschild said, in a statement to the British parliament in 1819, *"I care not what figurehead sits on the throne of England. The man who controls England's debt controls the nation, and I control that debt."*

This simple statement from not so long ago explains the true reason we continue to follow this path of destruction, allowing the financial industry to lead us to the slaughter. It also explains the enormous benefits to those who control the way your money is actually used.

The primary reason why no American political leader, or anyone in a position of authority, has rallied the American people with this message was also stated by Mr. Rothschild.

The few who understand the system will either be so interested in its profits or be so dependent upon its favours that there will be no opposition from that class, while on the other hand, the great body of people, mentally incapable of comprehending the tremendous advantage that capital derives from the system, will bear its burdens without complaint, and perhaps without even suspecting that the system is inimical to their interests. (The Rothschild brothers of London, writing to associates in New York, 1863)

What Mr. Rothschild said so many years ago is basically this:

- People who profit from his system will certainly not oppose it.
- People who depend on borrowing from others can't afford to oppose it.
- The remaining people aren't smart enough to know there is a system.
- These same people will pay for its very existence without even knowing it.
- None of them will understand that the system is hostile to their very way of life.

The truth is, our personal financial situations are controlled by a system that is over 150 years old. In that time, companies have developed ways to make this system even more despicable than Mr. Rothschild probably could have imagined. I'm sure he would be proud, though, of the creative ways that have been designed to separate us from our money.

I know that none of us wants to admit we've been manipulated by anyone, but we have to face facts if we're ever going to break free. And the only way we're going to break free is to let our financial masters know that we will no longer stand for their manipulation.

We must have an economic revolution if we are ever to take back our nation, our personal financial security, and our freedom. Of course, I'm not recommending a violent revolution, but I am promoting what I call "The Financial Leadership Revolution."

I teach people how to take control over their own money and how to make it work for them. The first step in this process is to realize that they have lost control over where their money goes, and who benefits from their loss of control.

Once they do realize this, people get angry! They want to know how to revoke the permission they have granted others: permission to reap the profit from their hard work. Then they're ready to move forward and take back their finances, their buying habits, and their freedoms. Are you ready?

MONEY MANAGEMENT VS FINANCIAL LEADERSHIP

You must first understand the difference between management and leadership. We're all familiar with the term *Money Management*, but very few people have ever heard of *Financial Leadership*. This is because those who implement Financial Leadership—banks, insurance companies, and investment firms—don't want you to know there is anything but Money Management.

If you don't know there is an alternative to the way they want you to think about money, you won't ask questions. If you don't ask questions, things just keep flowing the way they want them to, and you continue to be enslaved to them.

Think of yourself as a manager on a production line. You (the manager) know that you will always produce X number of units, as long as the line has Y number of parts to assemble. You (the manager) never decide on your own to change the output of production.

You only make changes when someone in a leadership role calls down to the line and tells you to increase or decrease production. A manager follows directions and *reacts* appropriately.

Leaders, on the other hand, anticipate change, often initiate change, but always wants to benefit from change. When leaders want to see a different result, they take action because they are in control. They act in a *proactive* way by telling others what they want, and then the managers react to provide the desired results.

The American people (in fact, consumers all over the world) have adopted the Money Management philosophy, and so are enslaved to those leading them into or out of whatever economic situation the leaders decide: just like sheep following a shepherd.

Now let's get right into how you can start your own personal economic revolution and take back control over the money you work so hard to earn, with what I call the *Seven Indisputable Laws of Financial Leadership*.

Remember: when people let money work hard for them, they get wealthy. When they work hard for their money, they just get tired.

THE SEVEN INDISPUTABLE LAWS OF FINANCIAL LEADERSHIP

LAW # 1: THE LAW OF ACCESS
Who is your money truly working for?

The *Law of Access* teaches that *"the most valuable asset you will ever know is that asset which you need, but cannot get your hands on."*

Imagine being stranded in the desert, having to endure the torment of the sun beating down on you as you try to find your way to safety. As you begin to dehydrate, you would give everything you have for a cup of water. That water, then, is the most valuable resource in the world to you.

That's how it was during the run on the banks during the Great Depression. People would settle for pennies on the dollar just to have enough cash to be able to buy groceries for their family. Loans were called in and homes were foreclosed on, all because people could not get to their money.

This is how it will be when hyperinflation hits us here in America, when people are once again struggling to simply provide for their families.

As I discussed in section 1, the Federal Reserve is artificially devaluing our currency, so your hard-earned dollars have less buying power every day. The value of our US dollar is shrinking to the point that it will only buy a fraction of what it used to. You see this in a combination of lower quantities and higher prices. A 5-pound bag of sugar may now only be a 4-pound bag, but the cost is the same; or the package that used to contain a pound of bacon now only contains 12 ounces, but the price is $1.50 more than you used to pay. Inflation is growing everywhere from the grocery store to the gas pump, yet our homes are only worth a fraction of what they were a few short years ago.

Employers are daily moving our jobs to foreign nations in order to escape the high taxes and uncertain government regulations on everything from health care to labor laws and safety legislation. No matter the reason for them leaving, these companies leave behind millions of people searching for new jobs—or just trying to figure out what to do next.

It seems like the only thing constant about financial issues these days is change. Times are changing rapidly and not always for the better. So how do we prepare for such times? How do we adapt to the future of what America will become? How do we prepare for job loss, or reduction in wages, or higher costs due to inflation?

This is why knowing the Law of Access is so important. Money is only good if you can get to it.

For example, you could have $300,000 of equity in your home when you lost your job. You might have been sending all your extra money to the bank to pay down your mortgage, and extra to pay off your credit cards, and still more to pay off your car. All the while you thought, "as soon as I get these debts paid down, I'll start building my retirement account."

Then change came, and you lost your job. Most people think

they can simply go to the bank and get a home equity loan, or refinance their mortgage to access some of that money, right?

Not so fast.

What's the one thing you need when you apply for a loan? That's right: a job, or the ability to repay. Without a job, you don't have access to any of your home equity.

What's even worse, banks will typically foreclose on houses with large amounts of equity faster than those with little or no equity in them. That's because the bank has gotten most of their original money back from you, and they know they could sell your house for less than the true value and still make a profit on the property.

This is one of the biggest mistakes people make with their money: they give every spare dollar they have to someone else to pay off debt, without thinking that that debt might actually work to their own benefit. They have been brainwashed by the banks and entertainers selling their one-size-fits-all, debt-free philosophy.

That's right, I said some debt can be good for you: a mortgage, for example.

Think about it: what are the only two tax deductions we're still allowed to have on our personal income? Our dependent children and the amount we paid to our lender for mortgage interest. If you didn't have these deductions, how much more would you have to pay in taxes this year?

Here's another way to look at it. If you owe $30,000 to credit card companies, $40,000 to banks for car payments, and $100,000 for your mortgage, you have a total of $170,000 in debt. The problem is that only the interest paid on the mortgage is deductible from your taxable income.

Another problem is that the higher interest rates you typically pay on the $70,000 for credit cards and car payments cause your monthly obligations to these companies to be higher than what you pay on the $100,000 you pay for your house. So you pay about 50% more interest per month on only 40% of the debt.

I understand the theory behind getting a 15-year mortgage instead of a 30-year, but there are much better ways to accomplish the same goal.

Here's one example of how we need to think of our mortgages as a financial tool, instead of simply as a debt we need to eliminate as soon as possible. Let's say you have $90,000 equity in your home, because you've been paying extra, in an effort to pay it off as soon as possible.

What if you refinance your house while you are still working, and obtain a 30-year mortgage which reduces your monthly obligation to the bank? You borrow enough to pay off all your non-preferred debt, thereby making all your interest payments now tax deductible. Your debt is still the same amount it was, $170,000, but now your monthly obligation has been reduced dramatically, and you have more tax deductions at the end of the year.

Looking at the numbers, here's how it all breaks down. Your mortgage payment was $1097.75 per month ($165,000 at 7% for 30 years). Your new monthly payment—since interest rates have dropped—is only $912.60 ($170,000 at 5% for 30 years). You just saved $182 per month on your mortgage payment.

The bigger saving here though, is the money you used to send to the credit cards and car payments. You have now saved approximately $800 per month on credit card bills and $600 on your car payments. That's a total of $1,400 per month that you were sending to creditors: expenses that offered you no benefit whatsoever!

Now you can put that entire $1,400 per month to work for you, instead of it working for someone else. You still owe the same amount, but you've allocated the debt in a way that benefits you instead of your creditors. Remember that creditors are in it for themselves, not for you; you are simply a number to them—so why would they tell you how to take charge of a situation like this?

If this is confusing, think of a bank or mortgage company as being like a restaurant. A restaurant only has a certain number of tables where they can sit patrons. The faster they turn those tables, or in other words have one customer finish so they can sit another patron, the more money they can make with that same table.

Banks are the same way. The sooner they can convince you to send them more money to pay down your debt, the faster they can lend it back to you or to someone else. Then they can make even more money off those same funds.

It's that simple, but I bet no one has ever told it to you that way before. Why wouldn't they want us to know? Because regular people like you and me aren't supposed to know these things. That's how the wealthy get wealthier; the less we know, the better they like it.

That's why they pay those entertainers so much money: to get you to send all you can back to the lending institutions, with the idea that you will save so much more money with a 15-year mortgage than a 30-year (for just one example).Let's take a quick look at our previous example, where we saved the couple $1,400 per month. If they take that same money they were sending to creditors every month and instead invested it, even earning merely 2% interest compounded annually, *in only 8 years* they will have $145,861 in savings: more than enough to pay their home off, if they want to. Now that one-size-fits-all advice of a 15-year mortgage doesn't sound so good, does it?

The important thing is that the couple had access to every dime of that money if they needed it for an emergency or in case of a job loss, or even if they just needed to replace their car. People who have access to and control over their money will always prevail during challenging economic times.

If you don't feel you're in control of your money, you are likely operating on the Money Management philosophy. That's when your money (or lack of it) is controlling you; that's when you are merely reacting to financial circumstances or the orders of your bank and credit card company.

Throughout this book, I will teach you how to stop using Money Management. Instead, you will be empowered to implement Financial Leadership, thereby taking control over your money and causing it to work for you, so you don't have to work so hard for it.

I do want to caution everyone about a serious issue facing many people who are sincerely trying to prepare for difficult times. This is the issue of being "gold rich, but cash poor." I know some people who have hoarded gold and silver coins and bars to the point that all their money is tied up in precious metals. This is the same phenomenon I saw in the 1990s when people were buying real estate hand-over-fist, so much so that all their wealth was tied up in property. But then when they suddenly needed cash, they either had to sell some property or borrow against it.

If I could offer everybody just two words of guidance they would be, DON'T PANIC! I've been telling people for quite some time that being prepared for challenging economic times means more than just having a stockpile of precious metals. In the next session, I'll talk more about this issue and offer some guidance about retirement account such as 401(k) and IRAs. (To stay up to date on all the latest financial information from around the world and get the most reliable financial guidance available, go to www.rodney-ballance.com and join our free e-mail list.)

LAW # 2: THE LAW OF RETURN
Should I Save or Invest?

I've heard it time after time in my 20 years in the financial services industry. People get their retirement account statement at the end of each quarter, and they revel in how much money they made. What a jubilant time when the client sees how much money they started with at the beginning of the quarter, versus how much they have at the end of that three months. They get excited when they talk to their financial advisor, who tells them their account grew over 20 percent.

What I've noticed, though, is that these people rarely take into consideration how much money they contributed to the account, and how much was actual growth.

Let's say your account balance was $20,000 at the beginning of the quarter. We will assume that you contribute 5% of your annual salary to your 401(k) plan, and your employer matches 50% of your contributions up to 10% of your annual salary. For this example we'll use $75,000 as your annual salary.

Your 5% contribution—taken out of your check before you ever see it—equals $312 per month, or $937.50 per quarter and $3,750 per year. The matching contribution from your employer, 50% up to 10% of your salary, equals $156.25 per month, $468.75 per quarter, or $1,875 annually. (If you're in the 20% tax bracket, you would have saved approximately $62 per month in income tax, or about $748 per year. This isn't that important at this point, but later in this section I will show you how this impacts your accessible income in retirement.)

You and your employer have contributed a total of $1,406.25 over the past 3 months, increasing your account balance of $20,000 by 7%. And growth of 7% should make anyone happy, right?

Let's assume no contribution factors change for the next 20 years, and you're ready to retire. If you truly were receiving a true 10% rate of return on your money, the $20,000 you started with, plus your contributions, would have grown over the 20 years to $475,484. That's not a bad chunk of change, you're probably thinking.

But wait. The reality is that **you and your employer provided 70% of the overall growth shown**, through your own contributions. Then you have to take out the fees charged for providing you with these not-so-incredible returns.

So, since your account balance was actually only growing by 2.7% (plus your contributions), the real value will only be $181,243—much less than you had hoped for. Your investment company claimed you would earn $400,000 from your wonderful 401(k), but instead you earned less than half that much!

I know, you would typically receive salary increases over the years, which would have increased your contributions. The stock market is also always going up and down, so there's no real way to predict exactly how much money you would truly have in retirement. If this is your argument, you're right.

My question is this: why would anyone gamble with their retirement money, with no way to predict exactly what they would have left (when they either no longer desire to work, or for one reason or another can't work)? Yet millions of Americans do precisely this every day, because they're told it's the only way to outpace inflation and generate enough money for retirement.

But now let's take a closer look at what you would have earned, assuming you had saved the $475,484 I mentioned earlier. Let's look at the money you would truly have access to from this magical 401(k) retirement tool, when you do retire.

For the purpose of this example, let's look at the account as if you really did have the incredible returns that produced a total of

$475,484. Maybe using the larger number will make you feel a little better, because this is more in line with what others want you to believe. Let's also assume that the tax rate didn't change, and inflation stayed the same, since we're assuming your income or contributions were also constant. Let's also assume you've paid off your mortgage, and have no dependent children at home.

The first thing to remember is that you will have to pay taxes on the entire amount of money in your 401(k).

This means that if you take distributions of $2,500 per month, you will also have to pay around $500 in taxes every month. (Remember: always seek tax information from your personal tax adviser.)

In fact, when you look at the total accumulation of $475,484 within the retirement account, you would really only receive $362,814, because the rest of it, $112,670, goes to your business partner: the Internal Revenue Service. From the very first day you accept a tax deduction from your paycheck to invest in your retirement plan, you take on this partner. Their philosophy appears to be "pay me now, or pay me a whole lot more later."

To prove my statement, look at how much less you would have paid in taxes during those same 20 years with all the above-mentioned assumptions. If—instead of putting any money in a 401(k) and later paying $500 per month in taxes—you had simply paid your $62 per month in payroll taxes upfront, after retirement you would owe less than $40 per month in taxes—at most. And you probably had a tax refund each year worth more than the savings from your pre-tax 401(k) deductions, leaving you with little or no tax owed on your original income to begin with!

Understanding that without a 401(k) your tax burden would be minimal, if any, we see that the myth of having more expendable income by contributing to pre-tax retirement plans is just smoke and mirrors. Who is really seeing the most benefit from your pre-tax contributions?

Your employer sees a 7.65% direct benefit from every dollar any employee has deducted before taxes. That's how much they save in having to send to the government in matching FICA contributions. The salesperson who set up your retirement account benefits every month, by being paid various fees directly associated with your contributions.

Lastly, the IRS benefits the most. If you do the math, you'll see that the Internal Revenue Service collects more than 10 times the taxes on your withdrawal than they would have received if you had taken your money when you earned it!

This shell game perpetrated in the break rooms and conference halls across America is financially raping hard-working citizens just like you, people who just want to have a little bit of money to retire with and to live out the rest of their lives enjoying themselves after their working days are over.

But if this magic bullet known as 401(k) isn't all it appears to be, then what can someone do to prepare for their retirement years?

There are virtually no more retirement plans, unless you work for the government—and none of us know whether Social Security will be around when we need it. One tool you might want to check out is called a '412(i)', also named after a paragraph in the tax code and similar to a 401(k). The big difference with this type of account is that the IRS, the employer, and the broker who manages the account do not benefit nearly as much as the employee does.

Of course, when you derive the greatest benefit from a financial tool instead of them, the companies aren't going to be as quick to implement or advocate such a program.

One good thing about these plans is that you can actually access them, in some cases, before you turn 59 and ½ years old. This is great when you want to buy a new car, send a child to college, or make renovations on your home without having to borrow from a bank. This type of plan allows you, the person who earned the money, to have access to it when you need it without the red tape associated with a plan overseen by the government.

(If you'd like more information about 412(i) programs, or just want some clarification about your personal retirement plan, give us a call at the Financial Leadership Academy.

We'll either provide such guidance for you though our office, or connect you with a competent and reliable financial professional in your area.)

In closing, I'd like to ask you which of these three options you would have picked over the past 10 years as your investment/savings method. If you had $100,000 in cash, would you have placed your money in mutual funds tied to:

1. The Dow Jones Industrial Average?
2. The S&P 500?
3. A financial tool earning just 5% compound interest?

I'm always amazed to hear people convince themselves one way or another when they answer this question. Almost 90 percent of the time, people say they would have purchased mutual funds that closely reflected the growth of the Dow Jones Industrial Average. Almost no one ever settles for the 5% return.

Let's take a look at this for just a moment. First, we need to see what the market generated over the past 10 years. As of December 31, 2011, the Dow was up approximately 22% from December 31, 2001. The closing value on Dec. 31, 2001 was 10,021, and close on Dec. 30, 2011 was 12,217, an increase of 2,196 points, or 21.96%.

Your ending balance would have been $122,000, an

increase of roughly $22,000 over ten years. You're probably saying, "That's fantastic!"

Now let's see how much you would have gained on that same $100,000 in the S&P 500 during that same time period. The S&P 500 was at 1,257 December 31, 2011, almost a 10% increase over the 1,148 close on December 30, 2001.

Your ending balance would have been roughly $110,000 over ten years. Again, you'll probably say that at least that's better than the 5% option. But is it really?

Let's take a closer look at earning 5% compound interest during that same time period on that same $100,000. According to the mathematical equation that proves compound interest and allows us to accurately predict earnings, you would have earned a 64.32% return on your money over that same ten-year period.

Your ending balance would have been $164,320.

Now that little 5% rate of return doesn't look so little, does it? This is exactly why Albert Einstein said, "The most powerful force in the universe is compound interest."

So, would you rather put your money to work based on mathematical fact and the endorsement of a certified genius, or based on some charts and graphs put together by a salesman in a nice suit trying to separate you from your money?

But how can a small interest rate outperform the markets to that extent? Why has no one told me these things before? How can I start acquiring this type of return? Can I really grow my accounts this fast, without the volatility of the stock market?

This is a clear example of how the Financial Leadership Academy educates people about how money really works. As we always say, "people who understand interest earn it; those who don't, pay it." Now that you know how it can work for you, I hope you're ready to start earning interest instead of paying it.

LAW # 3: THE LAW OF TEAMWORK
What Should My Team Look Like?

Dr. John C. Maxwell once wrote, "Nothing of significance has ever been accomplished by any one person alone." Let's first try to tear this argument apart, shall we? How can he say that nothing of significance can be done by a single person alone?

What about Thomas Edison? He invented the light bulb, as well as a host of other inventions that changed our lives. What about Alexander Graham Bell? Certainly his invention of the telephone was a single effort. What about the ultimate individual effort, Jesus Christ?

Well, even though Jesus was the only man in history who probably could have done it on His own, He chose not to. He chose to surround Himself with 12 others who would share the work and expand His reach. Edison and Bell also had support teams.

And this makes sense. When we realize that we can only be in one place at any given moment in time, it becomes clear that **to multiply our results, we have to multiply the resources needed to create those results.**

What does this mean for me, and how does it relate to my financial situation, you might ask?

The answer is simple. Do you know everything about finances, and can you do everything that needs to be done? No; you must rely on someone else to help you, someone who has the appropriate licenses and access to financial products. This is true even for simple things such as setting up a checking account at the bank or placing an insurance policy on your home or automobiles. Retirement planning or any other long term financial planning goal typically requires someone with experience and training as well, if you want the best results possible.

OK, now we understand that we need other people to help us and there's no way we can do everything on our own: at least not if we want the best possible results. Let's now identify what our team should look like, how to work with our team, and who is the team captain.

Let's build our perfect financial team like the United States Olympic basketball team of 1992 was built and coached. Considered by many to be the single greatest sports team ever, this team defeated their opponents by an amazing average of 44 points per game! Not surprisingly, they eventually brought home the gold medal.

It's important to realize that each man was handpicked to play a particular role on that team, and each had a specific position to play. During their exciting streak of brilliant victories, you never saw one of the point guards playing the position of center, nor did one of the forwards try to play in the guard position. Each person had a specific job to do, and they did it magnificently; this enabled them to surpass all expectations. If any one of those great athletes had played outside their proper position, the results of their Olympic quest would undoubtedly have been much less.

So when designing our dream team to achieve financial "gold", we must make sure to hand-pick the right people for the right job, and let them all work within their realm of expertise.

You might think that you don't have enough money to worry about having anyone help you. You might also think that no one worth having would want to work with the little bit of money you have. But you might be surprised to learn how many professionals are happy to help people who really want to make a difference for themselves.

The first thing you need to remember is that you will only accomplish the goals that you truly believe you can reach. Your own perceived limitations will be the very dagger through the heart of your ability to surpass your boundaries.

Wanting to help others who are willing to help themselves is just human nature. So if you're willing to put forth some time and effort to get the process started, I guarantee you there are professionals who will be happy to be part of your "dream team." But who should you look for, and what are the positions you need to fill?

The first thing you, as head coach, need to do is identify the team captain. This person will be the catalyst who will help you identify other needed positions, as well as the right players to fill those positions. The captain should be someone who has played the game successfully many times before and who understands the importance of following a game plan.

So what position will the captain play, and where do I find that player? The primary position on your team, and where the team captain should be, is the financial advisor. This advisor, if worth their salt, will already have people with whom they work who can fill the other positions.

If your financial advisor has successfully designed plans for other clients and has a working relationship with other needed teammates, you will have a much easier time coaching them and keeping them working together for your desired results.

Having to connect professionals who have never worked together can be done, but there are always challenges (typically ego and trust issues) that take away from the cohesiveness you need to keep the machine running smoothly.

The captain of your team will help you, the coach, make sure everyone is playing as they should to run your plays effectively and to score every time. After all, if you don't score, there's no need to even play; we're in it to win it.

Your team captain also needs to have a keen understanding of how various financial tools work. They must understand how to effectively implement these tools to first build a strong foundation, and then be able to construct a strategy that includes all six elements of a successful financial plan.

A successful plan needs to be:

1. Simple
2. Proven Effective
3. In Written Form
4. Profitable
5. Measurable
6. Flexible

We'll talk more about how to establish a successful plan in the section on the Law of Understanding. For now, let's just understand that we need a game plan, we need all the right players in the position of their strengths, and each player needs to have a clear picture of our desired.

The second position to be filled is a certified public accountant (CPA) with experience in something other than filing tax returns. Your CPA must be forward-looking and able to identify potential hazards before you hit them, not tell you what to do to clean up the mess after the problem occurs. Anyone telling you what you should have done, after the fact, is absolutely worthless.

In fact, all the players on your team need to have this philosophy. I can find any number of armchair quarterbacks who can tell me what I did wrong after the fact. We must surround ourselves with people who already recognize where the potholes are, and who can steer us clear of them.

Having a competent CPA for your captain to have access to while designing your plan will also be extremely advantageous as time goes on.

The third position on your dream team is that of a good attorney. Your attorney may or may not be involved in the game from the first play, but they will be instrumental in making sure you reach your long-term plans, and that everyone is following the rules.

Your attorney's primary function is to make sure that everyone knows and follows all the rules of law, and that everything is done in accordance with your goals. Your attorney might recommend such strategies as implementing a trust: revocable or non-revocable, for example. If your plans involve going into business, your attorney might recommend that you incorporate.

Once your team captain has identified some potential teammates, you should schedule a team meeting to make sure everyone is a good fit. You, the coach and owner, have the final say in who plays, and who sits on the sideline.

If—for any reason—you are uncomfortable with any one of your potential teammates, you should immediately inform your team captain, and have them find another player for that position. Your team will be with you for a long time, and you will interact on many different levels over the years. It is crucial that everyone respect each other, and that no one believes they are more important than the team as a whole.

I emphasize this because all too often the coach and owner (that's you) is intimidated by the attorney or the CPA, and they simply follow suggestions without understanding. They also blindly follow the advice of their financial advisor, without understanding what strategies are recommended or why.

Have you heard the term *player coach*? That's exactly what you have to be. You have to be engaged with your team. You must make sure that each of these players explain to your satisfaction what they are doing, why they're doing it, and what the expected outcome of that strategy will be. They also need to deliver an effective timeline to you so you can measure the overall success of the team's efforts.

If the team doesn't measure up to your expectations, replace the players who are not performing. Never let the team run you; you must run the team. A good leader will give authority to their subordinates, but the subordinate must understand that with that authority comes great responsibility as well.

Now let's clarify what to look for in your team captain: the certifications or designations you should require for your team leader. I was vague on this earlier, because there are some extremely worthy advisors out there who don't possess fancy designations or certifications. These professionals may have spent decades helping people do exactly what you want done, instead of paying for titles that only serve to impress.

I say this because I often hear from clients who are seeking to hire someone with a particular designation, such as CFP (for "Certified Financial Planner"). But do you realize that young people can now graduate from college as "Certified Financial Planners"—without having spent one single day actually working with a client?

I don't know about you, but I would rather have someone who has actually driven down the street they are trying to get me to drive down. It's like the blind leading the blind in most of these situations.

Here is a list of things you should look for when determining who will lead your team:

- They have actually done what you want them to do.
- They have relationships with others who can fill the positions of your team.
- They provide references of people like yourself whom they have helped.
- They understand the importance of a good financial foundation.

- They have the necessary license(s) to help you set up your plan.
- They have a clean record with your state's department of insurance and FINRA.
- They are part of a professional organization that promotes professionalism, such as NAIFA.
- Above all, make sure they are CFLA-certified through the Financial Leadership Academy.

Working with professionals who have graduated from our 16-module certification course will guarantee that you have made the right choice. Our rigorous standards, as well as our teaching and testing strategies, ensure that everyone who successfully completes our certification requirements will do a wonderful job for you.

Having the right team in place, the right people in the right positions, all working to help you reach your goals, will help you rest peacefully at night, knowing that your money is working hard for you. These professionals on your team will build and manage your plan so the money you need will always be there when you need it, and so you don't have unnecessary tax burdens or penalties.

If you need help finding that one perfect team captain, or any other member for your team, let us know. We have relationships with an extensive number of the very people who can help you make all your financial goals a reality.

LAW # 4: THE LAW OF TIMING
Don't Gamble With the Grocery Money

I believe Kenny Rogers said it best, in his hit country music song "The Gambler", when he told us, *"You've gotta know when to hold 'em, and know when to fold 'em."* If you have any money at all tied to the volatility of the stock market, this phrase certainly rings true to you.

Knowing when to play your cards and when to get out of the game is crucial. I know, I've heard it a million times: "But I have a guy who watches out for my investments. My guy says that I just have to ride out the storms, because my investment timeline is long enough to absorb some downside risks."

If this sounds familiar to you, please remember this one tidbit of information that may change forever the way you view investing: **your advisor only makes money when you invest the way he suggests**. If you move your money, he loses money, but if you keep it where it is and "ride out the storm," only you lose money. As long as you continue to pay them fees for using your money, they will be your best friends.

All these salespeople know is what their company tells them. They get memos each week telling them the mutual funds to sell that pay the highest fees and commissions, or earns them an all-expense paid vacation. Accompanied with these memos are graphs and charts that will "wow" you with the earnings potential.

But these guys will always follow their presentation with this line: "Past performance is no guarantee of future results." In layman's terms, this means "Buyer beware." In other words, at the moment those words are spoken, you're supposed to forget everything else the salesperson has said. Suddenly all their graphs and charts are no longer applicable, because now you've been warned that you could lose money.

Think about it: if you have any money in mutual funds at all, when was the last time the guy who sold them to you called to tell you to sell anything? If he did call, it was to tell you to weather the storm, or that a new opportunity had just come to light and he didn't want you to miss out on it.

I share my opinions with people all the time, and I let them know when it might be a good time to move money to the sideline for a while. When I mention that certain economic issues are troubling, and I'm doing this or that with my own assets, people usually act to protect themselves.

But some people don't act, because their advisor told them to "just hang in there." A friend of mine who works for a large retail company had a "hang in there" situation. On May 2, 2012, my friend asked for my thoughts on the market and what he should do with some money in mutual funds through his 401(k).

I told him if I were in his shoes, I would immediately move my assets to the interest-bearing account within his retirement account, because there was trouble on the horizon. I was referring to the potentially-troubling jobs numbers from April; also, European elections were about to be held that could severely stir the pot of the European debt crisis.

In addition, wealthy investors have an old saying: "sell in May and go away." This is because summertime is vacation time for the wealthy, so the novice investor should never have their retirement funds subjected to the volatility of the markets when the volume is particularly low, and when the only people playing the games are the ones who have no personal assets on the line. Remember, fund managers and brokers play with money they didn't have to earn: yours!

Well, my friend "just hung in there," and over the next several weeks he lost over 6% in that account because of his inactivity.

The whole point of investing is to buy low and sell high. Then why would you just let your money sit there, hoping that someone else will take care of it for you?

I learned a long time ago that no one will ever take care of your stuff as good as you will. I guess we sometimes don't believe that, though, because we've been sold the idea that these guys who sell us our mutual funds somehow know more about everything than we do.

But that's like saying the guy you just met at the blackjack table knows more than you do, so you should give him all your chips, then sit back and watch him play with your money. You hope he wins more than he loses, but when he's down to only $10 he tells you to give him more, and you do it! Why would you do that?!

The days of "buy and hold" are over, except for some individual stocks that pay handsome dividends. One sure fact you can count on: the guys who sell you your 401(k) or 403(b) or IRA or some other retirement fund are definitely not the ones you need to be listening to about the timing of your trades. Instead, always seek outside advice and solicit opinions from people who have nothing to gain from your decisions.

Just like my friend who lost over $30,000 from his retirement account in just 30 days, you may have lost money too. You must understand that having an interest-bearing account to use as a safe haven in troubled times only makes sense.

Knowing when to get into and out of the market is not something to take lightly. In fact, there are a great number of people who I would recommend to never get into the stock market at all. If you wouldn't take your money and lay it on a gaming table in Las Vegas, don't put it in the stock market: it's that simple.

I say this because everything in the market today is treated as a big game, and this game is all about the "bigger picture" of "return on investment" for the investment firms and big banks. It's not about the little accounts, like yours or mine.

Wall Street doesn't care if your 401(k) lost 30% this year, as long as hedge funds and banks made a profit. Oh yeah, most often their profit is the fees you pay from your 401(k) and other accounts while they're losing your money.

Knowing when to hold your assets and when to sell your assets is a tricky business, but it should never be treated as a game. So take a look at your retirement accounts and ask yourself, *"Do I really understand this investment? Do I fully understand where my money is, and who I'm paying for what?*

You should also ask yourself, *"If the stock market completely crashed tomorrow, would I have enough money to accomplish my goals <u>without</u> the money I've invested?"* If you wouldn't, then you're playing games with your grocery money, and you need to review your overall plan.

We don't build our homes without also building a solid foundation that we know we can count on for the long term. Why do we try to build our financial future without a solid foundation we can always count on for safety?

Here are some guidelines to see if your foundational financial tools are truly safe:

- Is there risk of loss?
- Are there potential penalties or fees assessed if I need to access this money?
- Will I need to ask permission to be able to use any of this money?
- If I am sued for anything, is money in this account subject to litigation or judgments?

If you answered "yes" to any of these questions, your money is not in what I consider an approved foundational tool. An approved foundational tool is one that protects you from loss, with returns that are guaranteed. You never have to pay a penalty to get to your money, nor ask anyone else for it.

Most important, you must make sure you can't lose your money if you're sued for anything. We live in a very litigious society today, where people will take you to court for basically anything. Lawyers get rich while others pay the bill.

Did you know there are only two financial tools in existence today that are protected from lawyers? In most states the only two truly safe financial tools are cash value life insurance, and annuities. One reason for this is that the wealthiest people in America use these tools as the foundations of their financial portfolios.

Tools like these were used by O.J. Simpson to avoid having to pay millions of dollars in damages after being found liable in the civil suit resulting from the death of his ex-wife and her boyfriend.

I had dozens of people ask me why O.J. could afford to play golf every day when he owed millions in judgments.

I simply told them that O.J. had someone like me set up the right tools for him early in his career, just in case something like this ever occurred.

Of course, no one could have seen the exact trouble O.J. found himself in, but even a car crash could result in you losing all your retirement money if you don't have the right tools in place to protect yourself.

It's not just the volatility of the stock market that requires good timing. Obviously, your initial planning has to be done in a timely manner as well. The earlier the better is always the right choice, but sometimes you don't know certain things until you read a book like this. In that case, I agree with the old saying: never put off until tomorrow what you can get done today.

I do hope this book has been helpful to you and that you find value in the message. More important, I hope the information you have gained from these pages will give you enough knowledge to call the person who "manages" your money and tell them that you are going to start taking a more active role in where and how your money is invested.

If you'd like some unbiased guidance, join our free email list at www.rodneyballance.com, or friend us on Facebook at Financial Leadership Academy. We'll send you regular updates about things to be careful of, as well as opportunities you might want to take advantage of. We will always recommend that you start with a firm foundation, before you subject your hard-earned dollars to any risk at all.

LAW # 5: THE LAW OF UNDERSTANDING

"Sales" simply means separating you from your money

As long as there have been people with assets, there have been other people who wanted to get control of those assets.

The sales industry is the single largest industry in the world, so it's no surprise that companies would dedicate the largest portion of their operating budgets to develop and enhance their sales team. Companies spend billions and billions of dollars each year rewarding their sales teams with lavish all-expense-paid trips to luxurious destinations, as well as beautiful and expensive gifts. These companies know that the more they reward their sales staff, the more sales they can expect from them the next year.

It doesn't matter if these salespeople are selling widgets, tires, freezers, or financial products. The more profit there is in the product being sold, the more valuable the rewards and incentives to the sales staff. My wife and I have enjoyed numerous trips all over the world, luggage, golf clubs, apparel, and even camping equipment from the companies I've sold for over the last 20-plus years.

The reason you will never hear any of this from people who have been successful at selling products is that they want to continue being successful at selling. If you knew the inside information you might not buy, and they would lose the nice stuff they get for selling you things.

I never looked at my job as being sales, though, because I was simply filling a need my clients had—and filling it with a trusted and reliable product. Now I understand that that is the basic definition of the word "sales".

Even at your doctor's office you're being sold things. The last time you were at the doctor's office, did they order some tests that you or your insurance company had to pay for? Was there a prescription given for some medication? If you visited the eye doctor, did the doctor provide an in-office store of frames and lenses? For your convenience, they made it possible for you to get what you needed right at their office.

Because of the increasing demand by the companies for higher and higher sales figures, though, the sales game has evolved into a competition to see how many people the salesperson can trick out of their money. So it's no wonder that salespeople are often the highest-compensated personnel in any organization. Without salespeople no product could be sold, and no money could be separated from the people who earned it.

With this understanding, let's turn to how these valuable salespeople are trained and why you need to understand all this. If you know how you will be targeted, you can avoid becoming a target. You already know this, I'm sure, because you probably never visit a used car dealer unless you absolutely have to; you know there's going to be a salesperson there, and you don't want to be sold.

I've personally trained hundreds of salespeople. Now I'm going to give you a clear understanding of the strategies these (mostly good) people use to lure you into their web of illusion. I purposefully call it their "web of illusion", because almost every salesperson in the marketplace today has been taught, "Sell the sizzle, not the steak." This phrase has been the mantra of every sales organization I've ever been associated with.

When the salesperson can get you to visualize yourself using their product, and to imagine how much better your life would be when you take advantage of the opportunity they've shown you, they know they have you.

Why does a car salesperson ask you if you'd like a test drive? Why does a cutlery salesperson in a live demonstration at your favorite market ask you to cut something to see how well the knife works? If they can get you to place yourself in the driver's seat of any product, you'll convince yourself that you can't live without that product.

You've probably ordered something from an infomercial at one time or another because the person demonstrating the product made you feel that your life would be improved if you only had that product.

The three words I just used are the key to the sales game: "made you feel." People buy on emotion, and then justify their purchase by rationalizing their decision. Marketers understand that they must cause you to have some type of an emotional response, if they have any chance of selling their products.

Take, for example, the hugely popular commercials shown during the Superbowl of American football. It's a fact that companies who advertise during the Superbowl always realize a significant boost in sales the day after the game, particularly if they made an online offer. (That's why it costs millions of dollars to advertise on these games.) It doesn't matter if the commercials make you laugh or cry, scare you, or provide a feeling of euphoria: they are successful because they invoke some type of emotion.

When was the last time you consciously sought out anything (except maybe gas for your automobile) without feeling that the product would make you healthier, wealthier, or wiser?

Companies know that everyone wants to improve their lives.

So what better marketing strategies than those which cause you to seek out their product over their competitor's because you believe their product will better improve your life, in either the realms of health and fitness, financial status, or enhanced knowledge?

Salespeople will often take this strategy beyond legal and ethical limits, though.

A family member recently was looking into some financial investments. He put the word out that he had a significant amount of money to invest. Suddenly every mutual fund salesperson, banker, and insurance agent was knocking on his door wanting to present their recommendations for his money.

One particular investment advisor, who represented a very well-known and well-established company, made an appealing pitch that caught our attention. After hearing exactly what this family member wanted to see in his idea of the perfect financial tool, the salesman started pitching a product that met every one of his requirements.

It was amazing that he was able to promise a guaranteed rate of return of five percent: exactly what this family member had wanted to see. The salesman was able to offer accessibility to the money in the exact time frame the potential client wanted, 4 years. The product had no apparent strings attached, and would have enabled the new client to watch his money grow with guarantees from the company, and then be able to walk away with all that money with no risk or potential for loss.

The salesman had credentials, the backing of a very well-known company, and promised all the things the client was looking for, right down to the letter.

This made my family member extremely happy, and he was ready to sign up on the spot. Fortunately, this family member had agreed to let me review any potential investment he was considering before he committed to anything. He was anxious to show me this one, because he was sure it would be perfect for him.

His excitement soon turned into disgust and anger when I showed him the research I uncovered about his potentially-perfect investment opportunity. I learned that the company this salesman represented did not even offer the *type* of financial tool my relative had been shown, much less the actual product.

The salesman had presented a business card from Lincoln Benefit Life, a subsidiary of the Allstate insurance corporation. This is a very respected and trusted organization, with years and years of experience and customer satisfaction behind them.

The product he offered was actually from a much smaller company called Lincoln Life out of Syracuse, New York. It sounds like Lincoln Benefit Life, doesn't it? The big difference is that Lincoln Life has no affiliation with Allstate whatsoever, and has a less-than-desirable rating with A.M Best, an industry rating agency.

So the salesman was trying to confuse his potential clients into thinking that his company was a much better company, by using the bait-and-switch sales practice that has been around as long as the sales game itself.

To make matters worse, the salesman flat-out lied about how the product worked, and how accessible the money would be to the client.

The product this guy was trying to sell my family member was a *variable annuity*, meaning that his investment would only grow if the mutual funds—that is, the stocks—inside the annuity grew. But there are no guarantees in the stock market!

The truth was the only way my relative could earn the guaranteed 5% was if he also bought what's called a *lifetime income rider* with the annuity. "That's not such a bad idea," you're probably saying; but the kicker is that if my relative had purchased that rider, the only way he could then access any of his investment was to take a lifetime income from his annuity. He would never again have access to his funds, only a monthly paycheck—of whatever amount the company dictated.

This type of misleading and illegal bait-and-switch has occurred all over America, particularly with variable annuities and life insurance, and indexed annuities and life insurance. There is enough truth in the sales statements to cause you to listen to the sales pitch, which persuades you to purchase based on an emotional response; by the time you realize you were misled, ten years has passed and you have no recourse but to take what the company gives you.

The salesman who sold the product has probably moved on to another sales job, and you have no one to turn to for help, so then it's too late to understand what you bought.

The time to understand a product that will take time to produce results is before you buy it.

You probably do several days of research on automobiles before you ever purchase the one you drive home. You will spend hours reading reviews of digital cameras before you spend $200. But how long do you research financial tools? If a salesman piques your interest, or you hear an entertainer on the radio or television pitching a particular product, you should not immediately give that product credibility.

A reverse mortgage is one tool that has seen a huge jump in popularity over the past several years. Someone doesn't have enough money to retire, so they call a toll-free number that someone like Robert Wagner or Fred Thompson recommends on a commercial.

The popular entertainer adds a trust aspect to the sales pitch, and then they hit you over the head with the emotional factor about how you can retire without fear of losing your home or having to make a mortgage payment.

The truth is that these tools often have disastrous consequences several years down the road, because all these things are is loans backed by the collateral of your home.

When you sign over the title to your house to anyone else, you are at the mercy of that person or company as to how long you can stay there. What if you run into more financial trouble, when the lack of a house payment isn't enough to rid you of all your financial hardships? You can't borrow against the house for more money, because, technically, you don't own it any longer. You can't borrow from the bank because you have no collateral or a job, because now you're retired. You are stuck with no recourse. You can't even sell your house because, once again, it's no longer yours!

Financial decisions are not to be made based on emotion!

Never buy any financial tool or strategy based on how it makes you feel. Make sure you have a good understanding of exactly how the tool works. Talk with people who have used that tool successfully, and have the guidance of a financial professional who will not benefit from the sale of such a tool.

At the Financial Leadership Academy, we review products for people, help them gain a better understanding of what the product is, and how it will impact them in the short- and long-term. This is our consumer advocacy program. We even help recover money for people who have fallen victim to unscrupulous salespeople.

I remember helping a 73-year old lady in North Carolina who had been sold a variable annuity, with promises similar to the ones made to my family member, whom I mentioned earlier.

This woman had placed her trust in the salesperson because he said he was a Christian, and he worked for a large, well-known firm. The woman had not realized that her investment had any exposure at all to the stock market.

She had unknowingly placed her entire life savings, over $400,000, in mutual funds through the façade of a variable annuity, with a false promise that her money was guaranteed.

The Financial Leadership Academy worked with this woman, and within 90 days the company refunded her the entire amount—even though her account value had already decreased by over 8%.

If you have a good understanding of these things before you buy, you can't be taken advantage of. So I encourage you to join our e-mail list today, at www.financialleadershipacademy.com. Our e-mails will help you stay informed about the economy, as well as about various financial tools you may be tempted with when someone wants to separate you from your money.

If you have an investment you are unsure about, let us know, and we'll put our team of financial professionals to work helping you understand what you have and how it will affect you down the road. If we find that your investment is not what you thought, we will work to help you get your money back.

The best offense is a strong defense. Defend yourself by avoiding sales strategies that invoke an emotional response from you. Remember the following questions, and if you find yourself answering "yes" to any of them, be cautious in your purchasing decision:

- Does this presentation promise financial freedom?
- Does this presentation promise a healthier lifestyle with little or no effort on my part?
- Does this presentation promise unbelievable results with no risk?
- Does this presentation reflect the answers I think I want to hear?
- Am I confused about even the slightest detail of this presentation?
- Does the salesperson want me to make a decision on this purchase today?

If you answered "yes" to any of these questions, don't buy the product! The better you understand what you're doing now, the fewer regrets you'll have in the future.

The Law of Understanding says, "If you don't 100% absolutely understand it, don't buy it!"

LAW # 6: THE LAW OF NECESSITY
Prioritizing Your Financial Future

I recently met with a couple in their 60s. This couple has three children, ages 23, 21, and 19, all in college. The couple's concern was how to pay for college for all their children, as the cost was going to be in excess of $100,000 per year.

I shared with this couple the wise words of a former economics professor of mine. My professor said that when someone is faced with the decision of whether to (a) pay for their kid's college, or (b) fund their own retirement, they should ask the following question: "Had I rather my children sleep on my couch while they are going to school, or would I rather sleep on theirs while I'm retired?"

Many people today are faced with this same dilemma. How do I pay for my children's college? These same people are also looking for ways to pay off their mortgage faster, to afford a vacation this year, to pay for home renovations, and to buy a new automobile.

Does this sound familiar to you? If so, you need to step back and look at your decisions rationally, not emotionally, as I mentioned in the Law of Understanding. The same criteria come into play as you prioritize your monetary decisions.

In this section, I'll share with you ways to pay for college without having to sacrifice your retirement money. I'll show you how to pay your mortgage off without having to send extra money to your mortgage company or bank. I'll show you how to have access to your money, so you can afford a vacation or make those necessary home renovations.

You must first decide to take control of your money.

That's a simple statement, but it's often a difficult mind-shift. Most of us have been trained to think the way marketing strategists want us to think, so what I'm about to tell you may sound strange at first, but the numbers will not lie, and my strategies are based on rational thought, not emotion.

Step One:

- Lay out all your monthly bills on the kitchen table.
- On the left-hand side of a sheet of paper, list all revenue-generating activities that you do: everything that causes money to come into your household.
- On the right-hand side of this same sheet, list all the money that goes out of your personal economy every week. (We have a free tracking chart at www.financialleadershipacademy.com if you need it.)
- On a separate piece of paper, write down how much you spend every week on items or services that you buy throughout the week: items such as coffee, lunch, snacks, gas, etc. You may have very little control over the amount of money you bring in to your personal economy, but you have considerable control over how much goes out, and to whom. How many ways do you show to bring in money? How many ways are there that filter it out?

Step Two:

- Next to each bill listed, write a number from 1 to 10. Number 1 is the highest-priority expenditure, and 10 will be the expenditure that is least important to your survival. (More than ten bills may justify consolidation or elimination.)

*Do not include contributions to retirement plans, life insurance, or savings accounts in this list.

- Under this list write these words: **"I want to reduce the money I'm sending to other people!"**
- On a clean piece of paper, list all the items that could potentially make money for you: savings, retirement accounts, life insurance, etc.
- Under this list, write this statement: **"I want to cause all these things to make me more money!"**

Your first priority should be to increase the number of revenue-generating activities or opportunities, and decrease the number of expenses. Wealthy people have multiple streams of income. In fact, they find more ways to make money than ways to spend it. That's why they're wealthy!

Step Three:
- On yet another piece of paper, list the names of the recipients of all your expenses.
- Under this list, write out exactly how it makes you feel to have all that money going to people you will never meet. Don't be politically correct with your comments. You will be the only person to see this, and it needs to make a statement to you!

OK, now do you have a higher priority for putting more of your money to work for you? If so, we'll move on. If not, there's nothing I can say that can help you. Until you want to make more of your money work for you, it will always be working for other people.

HOW TO PAY FOR COLLEGE:

This is not going to be a popular part of the book for people who think that the only way their children will ever have anything is if the parents give it to them.

Of all the creatures God ever created, only human parents keep their children in the nest until they are twenty years old. Even reptiles that live to be over a hundred years old allow their offspring to venture out on their own at an early age.

Now don't get me wrong: I'm not saying we need to kick our kids out on the street as soon as they can walk. I'm also not saying we need to kick them out of the house the day they turn eighteen.

What I am saying is, the sooner we allow our children to experience real-life successes and failures, the better equipped they will be to stand on their own two feet.

My children grew up with the understanding that I wanted them to be successful and that I would always be there for them and support their endeavors. They also knew, from an early age, that I had no intention of paying for them to go to college so they could party and mooch off the system.

My oldest son earned a scholarship he learned about because the school system where we lived was searching for teachers, so they developed a relationship with a university that had a great teaching program. The scholarship was that the school system would pay for one hundred percent of my son's 4-year degree, if he would return and teach in that school system for 5 years. They also paid him a salary, with benefits, while he attended the university.

My daughter was identified as a gifted student in her sophomore year of high school, and so was offered an opportunity to attend a special state-funded school for science and math. She had to move there to live during her junior and senior years, but with that sacrifice she received a full scholarship to the state university, where she is now pursuing courses preparing her for medical school.

Our youngest son, now fourteen years old, also understands the importance of maintaining good grades and a lifestyle of excellence, so he too can qualify for programs that will either help him pay for college or offer other opportunities.

A couple of years ago, I was interviewed by the Christian Broadcasting Network about ways to pay for college without acquiring huge amounts of debt upon graduation. We did the interview at a small college in the Ozark mountains, near Branson, Missouri. (My wife is actually a graduate of this wonderful school—a debt-free graduate.)

While conducting the interview, I learned that there are many colleges across America that students can attend and get a great education, often without spending any money out of pocket! You can watch this interview and other videos on our website, www.rodneyballance.com.

The network where all these schools are listed is http://www.workcolleges.org, if you'd like to review some options. Or you can visit the website of the school where we did the interview, the College of the Ozarks (http://www.cofo.edu). Other ways to pay for college include, but are not limited to: military service, scholarships, and of course working to pay for it.

I learned at an early age that when someone earns something themselves, they value that more than if someone else gives it to them.

This seems to be a theory lost on today's youth, and unfortunately lost on parents as well. I know we all want our kids to have more than we did and a better way of life.

But how good will their quality of life be if we spend all our retirement money to pay their way through college, and then we have to live with them after they graduate, because we don't have enough money left to live on our own?

Hate me if you will, but simply prioritize the money you have, and ask yourself what is the rate of return on the money you would send to any university. The emotional ROI of your kid's education doesn't count. If you're confused about this, go back and read Law # 5, the Law of Understanding.

Another sure way for your kids to be able to go to the school of their choice is to allow them to work during the summers and on weekends while they are in high school. If they're spending their own hard-earned money, they probably won't choose an expensive school. Money is no more valuable to anyone than the person who earned it. All right, let's move on now before I get everyone mad at me.

EARLY MORTGAGE PAYOFF

Traditional wisdom and banks tell us that we need to pay off our mortgage early, so we must send more to the lender to pay down the principle. But we have to understand who is telling us these things.

Remember my first law, the Law of Access. I told you how to redirect some of your money from bills and other obligations toward accounts that were working for you. Here's a quick paragraph from that section to refresh your memory:

> *Let's take a quick look at our previous example, where we saved the couple $1,400 per month. If they take that same money they were sending to creditors every month and instead place it in a financial tool, even earning merely 2% interest compounded annually, in only 8 years they will have $145,861 in savings: more than enough to pay their home off, if they want to. Now that one-size-fits-all advice of a 15-year mortgage doesn't sound so good, does it?*

In this paragraph I alluded to another financial tool earning 2%. What if you could find a tool earning 4%, or 7%? Would you be interested in learning more about how that financial tool could work for you? I just moved some of a family member's money into a fixed rate annuity earning him 8.65%. How quickly could you pay off your mortgage at that rate?

Many of the primary financial tools I have used for my clients over the past three decades have been life insurance products, particularly whole-life insurance or fixed-rate annuities. One reason I use these tools is because they are among the only investments which have legal protection from litigation (in case a client was ever sued for anything).

How did O.J. Simpson go out and live the life of a multi-millionaire after losing legal battles that resulted in millions of dollars in judgments against him? He was able to do that because someone like me set him up with one or more of these tools at the foundation of his financial portfolio, early in his career.

A proactive approach to financial planning, before they have to react to legal issues, protects even the most despised individuals. Shouldn't these tools also work for good people like you?

We often don't allow these tools to work for us because we are taught that they are somehow bad, and we listen to paid mouthpieces tell us we should never use cash-value life insurance. But we're also taught by the same people that a 15-year mortgage is the only way to go.

With that myth already disproved, let's understand that you should not close your mind to these other financial tools. They were good enough for people like Walt Disney and J.C. Penney, and I'm confident they can be good enough for you.

I said this earlier, but it is worth repeating: If 10 years ago you had had $100,000, and you earned a 20% return on it over those

10 years, you would have $120,000 now. But if you had had the same $100,000 invested in a life insurance policy earning just 5% compound interest over that same 10-year period, you would now have $164,320, a 64% return.

Why do so many people fail to see the forest for the trees? Because we're told the forest doesn't exist—by the people who want us to focus on the trees.

When you make it a priority to understand how various financial tools actually work, and not just take for granted that someone else knows what they're talking about and has your best interests in mind instead of their own, you can significantly increase the amount of money you have. When you know that a seed will only grow if you actually plant it, and you ignore anyone who tells you it will grow if you just lay it on your driveway, then you will reap the fruits of your labor.

The same is true with financial tools: you must make it a priority to better understand how and why they work. I explained to you how salespeople work, and that their only priority is to separate you from your money. Now make it your number one priority to turn the tables on everyone else, by deciding to review where every dime of your money goes, and make as much of it work for you as possible.

I want you to view your various revenue streams as an orchard. Make sure the trees are always healthy, and producing delicious and desirable fruit. The more fruit-bearing trees you produce, the longer your needs will be satisfied from them.

As some of your fruit ripens, you take the seed and plant more fruit trees (think of earning dividends), thereby increasing your orchard and your production potential. You would never want to cut down your fruit-producing trees to use as firewood.

Your financial portfolio should be like your orchard. Make sure all your trees are producing fruit; eliminate the trees that aren't producing for you, and use them for firewood. Every time you give money to someone else, you're just burning it up as firewood, with nothing more than a short-term benefit for you.

LAW # 7: THE LAW OF MOTIVATION
Why Do I Do the Things I Do?

In the financial services industry, it's widely known that financial advisors do things for only one of two reasons: they either sell out of need, or out of greed.

That's it; there's no middle ground. I learned this during my training many years ago, when my manager and I were driving to our next appointment. He looked over to me and said, "Rod, as you start working on commission, you'll find that there will be times when you're desperate to make a sale to pay your bills. Don't let your desire for a paycheck get in the way of doing what's right for the client."

Those words have echoed in my head many times, and I pass on that principle to new advisors when I train them. I thank Harvey Bedsole for his wise teachings and his personal story that made such an impact my business and on my life, and thereby on millions of other lives all over the world.

A client looking to me for help in determining what to do with their money won't know that I might need the commission from their sale because I'm late on a car payment, or I need to pay the mortgage. One thing they should always know, though, is that I am recommending a product or service that will always be to their benefit, not mine.

Over the past decades working in this industry, I've met some salespeople who would sell their own grandmother a product because it would bring them the highest commission, even though they fully knew that it wasn't the right product for her.

I've also seen selfless acts from some magnificent advisors—acts that reinforced my belief in our business. In this industry I've met and prayed with some of the most honest and caring people I've ever known, and I am blessed to call them friends.

Some of these pillars of society are working with me now as ambassadors for the International Financial Leadership Association. These men and women display their motivation every day, as they volunteer to work with families all over America to help them understand how various financial tools work, and then implement strategies to help them achieve their financial goals.

Now let's see what some of these goals are.

Just as I've worked with some of the best and worst advisors in our industry, I've also worked with some of the best and worst clients. It has become quite evident to me that the motivation of the client usually determines the ultimate level of financial success they realize.

Like fire, money is one of the most useful tools we have, but also one of the most destructive. A fire out of control can burn down your home; money out of control can burn down your life. When people care more about building their bank account than the consequences of gaining that money, they can find themselves surrounded by leeches: people who are only there to get what they can from you.

On the other hand, I've seen people who simply want to provide for and protect their family. They use the money they've earned to enjoy time with the people they love and care about. These people aren't driven by greed—they are motivated by love.

When we are motivated by love to do the best for the people and organizations we care about the most, I believe God rewards our desires by multiplying our abilities and resources. I'm often asked,

"How much should I tithe to my church?" My reply is simple: "I have never worked with anyone who has been faithful in their tithing who needed help getting out of debt."

Most often, the people who support others with what they've been blessed with end up being blessed with even more. Good stewardship is critical in the life of a Christian, and that ideal should flow through the heart and mind of every one of us, regardless of our beliefs.

It's no secret, though, that one can be generous to a fault. I faced a dismal financial situation when I tried to run my business as a non-profit ministry. I was so thankful for what I had and the opportunities I was being offered, that I wanted to do everything for free for everyone.

I was spending so much of my time doing free work for people who called into my radio show, and helping people get out of their bad financial situations, that I was actually putting my own family at risk of financial hardship. There should be a mixture of charity in whatever we do, but not to the point of neglecting our own necessities.

I now operate a company designed to make a profit. I've learned that we can do a whole lot more good for others when I have the resources, than I ever can when I'm worried about paying my bills.

Which brings me full circle to what I said about need vs. greed. Whether you're a licensed financial professional or a client of one, you must regularly ask yourself, "Why do I do what I'm doing? Am I making this decision based on my personal mission statement, or just for a quick buck?"

What's that, you don't have a personal mission statement? Don't feel alone my friend, most people have never thought about having such a thing. Now you might be asking, "Why would anyone need a personal mission statement? I thought those were only for companies?"

Why do companies have mission statements? They place these two- or three-line statements everywhere their employees or customers are, so the whole world can see why they do what they do.

You can see the Financial Leadership Academy's mission statement at the top of the home page of our website. Our mission statement is: *In an effort to please our Creator, we will fill the public's need for accurate and reliable financial information, and connect them with competent and accountable financial professionals.*

We place our mission statement prominently so those who know nothing about us can know what we do and why, and within a few seconds. Our mission statement also serves to keep our direction focused and our mission clear.

If we ever start to veer off the path of what this organization was founded to do, we can correct our direction and get back on course because we know our *true north*. That's the underlying reason every company has a mission statement: to always know the direction they should go.

The same is true for individuals. If you have a clear mission statement for your life and you write it down, you can always measure whether or not you are heading in a direction that's in line with your overall mission in life, or if you're moving in a dangerous direction.

I don't know the reasons you have for doing the things you do, but one thing is true: doing the right thing is always the right thing to do!

I met with a couple recently who shared their financial portfolio with me, and asked me how they could make more money. They were afraid that what they had wouldn't last long enough for a comfortable retirement. I made some comments about some of their investment choices, and told them they could make more money if they owned a few other specific stocks.

Their reply was refreshing. Almost simultaneously they said, "We don't want to invest in any company that supports or promotes behavior which is contradictory to our beliefs." They obviously knew their true north and were not willing to veer off course, not even for the promise of higher returns on their money.

That's what having a personal mission statement does. It keeps you in line with who you are. These people are so focused on doing the right thing, they will never be derailed.

I shared some thoughts on how they could accomplish their desire to have more money in retirement without compromising their faith. There are ways to accomplish your financial goals without just following the herd. Just because you know someone who says buying Z is what everyone should do, that doesn't make Z right for you.

Next time someone tells you about an idea for getting rich or multiplying your cash, ask yourself this question: Is this idea in line with my core beliefs, and does it fit my personal mission statement? If it doesn't match who you want to be, simply say thank you, and walk away.

I've made many mistakes in my life. Some of those mistakes were because I turned away from my true north. I have done things in my life that I'm embarrassed about and even ashamed of. The only good thing that ever comes from making mistakes is what we learn from them, and how we use what we learned to help others.

I pray that the words I've provided you in this book will help you avoid some of the mistakes I've made, and keep you on track to accomplish all your financial dreams. If I can ever be of assistance to you, please don't hesitate to contact me at the Financial Leadership Academy.

To sum up the Law of Motivation: "For every action there is

an opposite and equal reaction." From a Biblical perspective this would be: "What we sew, we also will reap." What motivates you to do the things you do: need or greed?

THE GOLD RULE

I JUST HEARD MY RECEPTIONIST field yet another call from someone who had seen me on television. They called in to ask where they should buy gold. The caller stated that they understand the only way to survive the imminent economic collapse is to have all their assets in gold or silver.

Friend, please hear me loud and clear. Buying gold is not always the answer. Remember, you should never listen to a one-size-fits-all philosophy when it comes to your money. This is a perfect example of what I was telling you. Historically speaking, by the time normal hard-working people hear about any great investment, the real money has already been made.

Just as in any other commodity trading, dealing in precious metals is dangerous and can cost you dearly. Buying low and selling high is the mantra to follow for all investing. Gold saw a tremendous increase in value during the economic crisis of 2008 – 2011. People who had purchased gold in 2007 for around $800 per ounce saw the value of their assets increase to around $1,900 per ounce (before the government changed the rules, causing the value to crash to around $1,600 overnight.)

Those who bought this volatile investment at its height—because that's what everyone else was doing—actually *lost* huge amounts of money.

Just as with trading in any other commodity, you have to know what you are doing and why, or you can lose your shirt. The investment might turn a profit eventually, but it might be decades before that kind of growth will be seen again.

In this section, I'm going to go into some detail explaining how some financial tools work, and how you can cause them to work for you. We'll also uncover some bad information that is being dispersed that could actually cause you to lose everything.

Before I dive into this, though, let's just remember what I said earlier, about how important it is to not follow the one-size-fits-all mentality. Try to remove all your preconceived ideas about personal finance and just allow me to teach you. I have nothing to gain by causing you to think in any certain way. I just teach; I don't sell.

In this session, we'll take a look at five different financial tools, as well as precious metals. I'll explain how each of them works, and how they can benefit you or hurt you, depending on how you choose to use them.

We'll look at stocks, bonds, mutual funds, life insurance, CDs (Certificates of Deposit), and annuities to determine the benefits and drawbacks of each one. Having a better understanding of how each of these tools work will give you a better understanding of how to make some of them work for you.

These brief descriptions are meant to give you a broad overview, and should not be used to make specific financial decisions. Always seek guidance from a certified Financial Leadership Advisor. Allow them to help you coordinate your financial matters, to make sure everything you have is actually working to benefit you.

UNDERSTANDING STOCKS

A simple definition of *stock* is this: you give a certain amount of money to a specific company, and in return they provide you with a specific percentage of ownership in that company, relative to your investment. The more shares you own, the larger the stakeholder in the company you become. The more of the company you own, the more of a voice you have in decisions that shape the future of that company.

Many people today believe they can't afford to own individual stocks; and if they could, they wouldn't know which ones to buy in the first place. Many folks also have the idea that they have to be in the stock market if they are to see any real increase in their portfolio, so they rely on their 401(k) plan at work to grow their wealth.

The reality is, if you just look around at the products and services you use every day, you will see a plethora of stocks that would be good to own and that you could afford. If you use the company's products and recommend them to your friends, other people are probably doing the same thing, and the company is growing because of it.

The biggest misconception about buying stocks is, "I don't know when to sell them." People don't want to buy a stock that might go down in base value. An even bigger concern is how much the particular stock has increased in value over time.

What if I told you that these two concerns that everyone has… do not matter in the least!?

What if I told you that you can benefit more when a stock you own goes *down* in value than when it goes up? What if I told you that it doesn't matter how much the stock has increased in price over the past ten years? You'd think I was crazy, wouldn't you?

Here's the beauty of owning *dividend-paying* stocks.

Let's take a look at Coca-Cola, for example (trading symbol

KO). As I write these pages, this stock price is roughly $40 per share. Ten years ago that same stock sold for $26 per share. At first glance, you'd say that this was a bad investment, because the stock price only went up $14 per share over 10 years.

But the real value in this stock, or in any other dividend-paying stock, is in the *dividends earned* on each share of stock you own.

Let's assume that the dividends were constant over the entire 10-year period, at $0.26 per share. Let's say you bought 100 shares for $26 per share ten years ago and never purchased any more.

Let's further assume that you reinvested those dividends so they would purchase more shares of Coca-Cola stock every quarter, when dividends were paid out. Every three months, then, your dividends of $26 (100 shares x $0.26) were buying 1 new share of Coca-Cola stock.

So each year, you actually increased your ownership of this company by several shares. The first year you would have added 4 new shares. The second year those 4 shares were also reinvesting their dividends for you, causing your investment to be compounded.

Assuming the stock price never increased, and your dividends were always allowed to buy more shares of the stock, after 10 years you would have had a 48% growth in the number of shares of your stock. In other words, if you had simply allowed your original investment of 100 shares to continue growing on its own, after 10 years you would own 148 shares of Coca-Cola stock. (Naturally, we all understand that the price of any stock fluctuates, and dividends may or may not be consistent, but you see how you can effectively multiply your assets.)

If after those 10 years you were then to start using those dividends as income instead of reinvesting them, you would have increased your income potential by at least 48%—and even more if the stock price or dividend payout had increased.

The key is that you allowed that original money to work for you. You never contributed another dime to that stock, yet your "orchard" that we spoke of earlier continued to grow and produce even more fruit for you.

If you had not reinvested your dividends and so only had your original 100 shares of stock, the value of your total investment would only be worth $2,600. But because you allowed that investment to grow, your total investment would now be worth $5,476, a 102% return—plus future dividends.

Let me once again stress: the total price of your shares of stock is not the important thing, the earnings you receive in dividends are. You still keep your stock while you receive the dividends as income. So your asset value might remain constant, but you are receiving a regular paycheck every three months, which is the fruit that orchard is supplying you.

Here's the description page for Coca-Cola stock (symbol KO) from the Wall Street Journal's Marketwatch website, http://www.marketwatch.com.

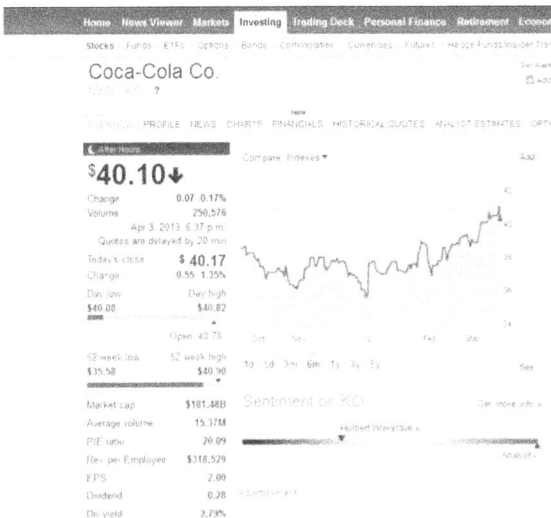

Looking at the screenshot above, notice that the current dividend per share ($0.28 in this case) is listed near the bottom left corner of the picture, right above the dividend yield, which is 2.79%.

If you are currently earning merely 1% on your savings in a bank, wouldn't it make more sense for you to let your money work harder for you, by instead purchasing some dividend-paying stock that pays you more?

But many people are afraid that the stock price will fall as soon as they buy it. Okay, let's assume that in the above scenario it actually did drop dramatically. Let's assume that, the day after you bought your Coca-Cola stock for $26 per share, the bottom fell out and the stock price was cut in half, to only $13 per share. Let's further assume that the price of that stock never recovered, and it's still worth only $13 per share today.

But as long as the dividends continued to be consistent, this would actually have been *good* for you.

Why? Because at the lower share price, the dividends of $0.26 per share would now buy you **twice as many shares of Coca-Cola stock!** So the number of your shares would double—and each of these shares would also be paying you a dividend, thereby multiplying your assets even more.

Instead of the 102% increase in asset value if the stock price had stayed constant, you would have seen **over 200% growth** from your $2,600 investment. As Albert Einstein said, the most powerful force in the universe is compound interest.

The same principle also applies if you own stock in a good company with solid leadership and a clear business model. (I share more about some companies that meet these criteria on my regular radio show and teleconferences with members of our Financial Leadership family.)

UNDERSTANDING MUTUAL FUNDS

Having a better understanding of what a stock is will now help you better understand what a mutual fund is. Mutual funds have been around since the 1700s, in one form or another. To quote James E. McWhinney:

Historians are uncertain of the origins of mutual funds; some cite the closed-end investment companies launched in the Netherlands in 1822 by King William I as the first mutual funds, while others point to a Dutch merchant named Adriaan van Ketwich, whose investment trust created in 1774 may have given the king the idea. Ketwich probably theorized that diversification would increase the appeal of investments to smaller investors with minimal capital.

The name of Ketwich's fund, *Eendragt Maakt Magt*, translates to *unity creates strength*. The next wave of near-mutual funds included an investment trust launched in Switzerland in 1849, followed by similar vehicles created in Scotland in the 1880s.[2]

Before 401(k) came into the picture, mutual funds were never used much in America because people enjoyed pension plans that provided a lifetime income for them upon retirement. These plans were funded in whole or in part by the employer for the full benefit of the employee, in recognition of a number of years of service to the company.

These old-style companies, who truly cared about their employees, used products like interest-sensitive annuities and cash-

2   James E. McWhinney, "A Brief History Of The Mutual Fund" (http://www.investopedia.com/articles/mutualfund/05/mfhistory.asp)

value life insurance to fund these pensions. Insurance companies that underwrote these financial tools were the only businesses able to guarantee a lifetime income for the employee.

When 401(k) came along, it was an easy escape for companies to get out of funding these pensions, and instead to dump the responsibility of planning for retirement directly on the shoulders of the employees. Companies went from rewarding their employees for their dedication and years of service to telling them, "You're on your own."

(If people notice that today there doesn't seem to be any loyalty to companies by employees, this is one major reason why. There is now practically no incentive to stay with any company for your entire career, which means that people are always looking for a better opportunity. The meaning of *commitment to a company* went from 20 years to giving a two-week notice.)

Anyway, back to mutual funds. The only reason I brought up 401(k) is because even the US government understands the importance of having access to and control over your money. Doesn't that sound familiar to you?!

Mutual funds became so attractive because, for the first time ever, hard-working Americans could save as little as $50 per month in an account sponsored by their employer, and have it invested for them. With that $50 investment each month, the employee was actually buying little bits of stock in several different companies at the same time. They were diversifying their portfolio.

One such mutual fund, Growth Funds of America, a product of the American Funds company, is actually made up of roughly 600 different companies. So if you had $50 taken from your paycheck this month and invested in that particular mutual fund, you would now own a small piece of 600 different companies.

But even if any of those companies paid dividends, you would never realize a benefit from them, because mutual funds are among the most expensive methods of investing there are today. If your $50 was divided equally between all 600 companies, you would own .08 (8 one-hundredths) of a share of each one of those stocks (assuming all stock prices were exactly the same.)

This is why I refer to mutual funds as the time-share of investments. You all know what I'm talking about. These days there are very few people who haven't sat through a 90-minute timeshare presentation just so they could get free tickets to an amusement park or some concert, or possibly even just a free breakfast.

When you purchase a time-share, you are buying one week's use of one apartment or condominium every year, in exchange for a certain price. For that same price, you could probably have bought a small house down the street and had access to it every week of every year, and even rented it out for additional income.

I don't want to criticize time-shares too much, though, because a lot of people own them and are very happy with the arrangement. That's all the more reason for my teachings: what's right for one person might be the worst thing in the world for someone else.

So why do so many people listen to those entertainers who sell their one-size-fits-all philosophy of mutual funds?

If you look at your retirement plan quarterly statement, you will find that it's made up of several different funds. Each of the individual funds is made up of hundreds of different companies. If you think your statement is confusing, though, you should try to find out exactly how many shares of any specific stock you actually own through your investments. That would drive you absolutely nuts.

I always tell people that there are no bad financial tools. But if there were to be one bad tool, mutual funds would certainly be a contender. The only thing worse than a mutual fund would be a variable annuity which holds mutual funds inside of it as the driving engine for growth. You would pay the high fees of the mutual funds, plus you would pay the higher fees associated with this type of annuity. Stay away from both of these financial tools!

If you only have $50 per month to invest in the stock market, either buy whole shares of stock in companies that cost $50 or less, or save your money until you have enough to buy a whole share.

Owning full shares of stock provides you with the full benefit of that stock. You can sell it, use it for collateral against a loan, or let it earn you dividends. Whatever you do with it, you benefit, because you maintain control over and access to your money.

UNDERSTANDING BONDS

When you buy a stock, you are actually buying a piece of that company. When you purchase a bond, you are actually loaning the company money, in return for a specified guaranteed rate of return in interest.Companies use your loan to expand their operations in an effort to reach more customers for their products, or to meet the demands of an already expanded demand for that product.

The other type of bond is a government bond, also known as a *municipal bond*, or *muni*. This loaned money has the same basic concept as a corporate bond, but in addition to providing you a guaranteed return at a specified interest rate, loaning the government money can have tax advantages, so that the growth on your money may be exempt from state and federal taxation.

Check with your tax professional to make sure that the specific bonds you might be interested in meet the requirements to provide you with that tax benefit. Your financial advisor should also be able to provide you with more information and guide you in acquiring some of these financial tools.

Remember: *"People who understand interest earn it. Those who don't, pay it."*

Special Note: As a bondholder of any entity, you are a creditor of that entity. If a company to whom you've loaned money goes out of business or files bankruptcy, you are at the top of the list of those who receive a payback of your money. Bondholders and other creditors are repaid before any stockholders receive any benefit from a closed or bankrupt company.

UNDERSTANDING CERTIFICATES OF DEPOSIT (CDS)

A CD, or Certificate of Deposit, is among the easiest of financial tools to explain. You typically purchase a CD from a bank. The bank will have various types of CDs, such as 6-month, 12-month, 36-month, and so forth. (The months simply refer to the amount of time you are giving full use of your money to the bank.)

You sign a form that signifies your agreement to pay the bank a certain sum as a penalty, should you require any of your money from that account before the term is over. The bank charges these fees to ensure that they will not lose any money.

When you lock up your money in a CD, the bank then invests that money somewhere that will produce a return for them. A CD is just another account at the bank by which they receive access to your money for a small obligation to you. They then use your money to increase their profit margin, once again proving that whoever has control over and access to your money will enjoy the benefits of that money.

Usually, the larger amount of money that you are willing to put into a CD, the higher the rate of return you can negotiate from the bank. Always make sure to negotiate, whether you're depositing money or borrowing money. The better rate you receive, the more your money is working for you, instead of for someone else.

UNDERSTANDING ANNUITIES

Annuities are provided by life insurance companies, not banks (unless the bank sells it through an insurance company). Just like a CD, with an annuity you also agree to give access to your funds to the issuing agency for a minimum amount of time.

One important difference with an annuity, though, is that you have access to up to 10% of your money every year—without paying a penalty. Having this access can be very beneficial to the annuitant (the owner of the annuity, in most cases).

Also, annuities are among the only 2 financial tools in existence that provide some measure of protection against litigation. If you are sued for injuries—for example, relating to an automobile wreck—the courts cannot get to any money that you have invested in an annuity. This feature alone makes an annuity a very appealing tool for anyone's financial foundation, and I am not aware of any state in America where this law does not apply. (But before purchasing an annuity, always consult with your primary care advisor for clarification of your specific product and situation.)

These days, there are actually three different types of annuities: fixed rate, variable rate, and equity indexed.

FIXED RATE ANNUITIES

Fixed rate annuities are the easiest of all annuities to understand. They are a contract between you and a life insurance company, guaranteeing you a minimum rate of interest that the company will pay you.

In addition to the minimum rate, the company will have often a higher rate that they are currently paying, based upon the profitability of the company as a whole. The more profit the insurance company makes, the more interest they pay to your account.

The great thing about a fixed rate annuity is that you cannot lose your money. There are legal safeguards in place that protect policyholders from losing their money, even if the insurance company goes out of business. Some experts say that these safeguards are more advantageous to the depositor than the FDIC protections afforded through banking institutions.

Fixed rate annuities are my favorite. Call me a traditionalist, but these tools have provided millions of people with lifetime pensions, even leaving money for widows after the annuitant died.

This is the financial tool used to fund the pensions you've heard about from the good old days: the lifetime income that people would be rewarded with after working for a company for twenty or thirty years. The employer and the employee (in some cases) would contribute to this account, which earned a *guaranteed* rate of return.

The life insurance company provided regular statements to the employee to inform them of how much money per month they would receive at any specific point in time. No one had to worry that their pension fund was going to lose value just before they retired: they knew to the penny exactly how much they would receive every month for the remainder of their life.

Employers would contribute to these accounts, on behalf of the employee, after a predetermined time of service. At some point, called vesting, the employee received ownership of all the funds in the retirement account. A company's vesting period was often 3 to 7 years or more, thus encouraging the employee to stay with the company.

If the employee left the company before they were fully vested, they could only carry with them the percentage of the account in which they were fully vested. For example, if you worked for a company requiring 10 years to be fully vested and you decided to leave after 5 years, you might only receive 50% of your retirement money, because you were only 50% vested.

EQUITY INDEXED ANNUITIES

The equity indexed annuity has the same basic features as the fixed rate annuity, except that there are few, if any, guarantees. Instead of your rate of return being a direct reflection of the insurance company's profitability, your return is tied directly to a particular equity index, such as the S&P 500.

Most equity indexed annuities do guarantee that you will not lose any money in case the index to which it is tied doesn't gain in value for the tracking period (typically twelve months). These products also provide caps to guard against the company having to pay you more than a certain amount during that same time frame.

For example, let's say you have $100,000 in an equity indexed annuity during a 12-month period where the S&P 500 posted a loss of 10%. Your account will actually be exactly the same at the end of the period as it was when the period began. You made no money, but you didn't lose any either.

Now let's say that the S&P 500 posted a 20% gain for the period in question. Most of these accounts have a cap of about 5–7%. So although you might expect to see your $100,000 grow to $120,000 at the end of the period, instead your account will only be worth $105,000, because your cap was 5%.

Annuities are wonderful and viable financial tools, but if you are going to invest in the stock market, *don't* do it through an annuity or a mutual fund. For this reason, I will only briefly mention the third type of annuity, *variable annuities*, without going into too much detail.

VARIABLE ANNUITIES

Absolutely the most confusing and expensive financial tool in existence, the variable annuity provides returns to the owner from the growth of the mutual funds located inside the annuity itself.

These volatile and highly dangerous financial tools are sold by slick salespeople because they make huge commissions from them. You pay the fees for the mutual funds located inside the annuity. Then you pay additional fees for the annuity itself. Plus, you are almost always sold additional features to "protect" you. These additional features are called *riders*.

A rider you might see on one of these annuities is a *lifetime income rider*. Once this particular rider is placed on your annuity you will have no control over your money, except by paying a huge penalty. Even worse, the rider states that you surrender all access to that money once the lifetime income has started.

You are often tricked into having this rider because it's the only way the salesperson can make this financial tool sound attractive. By accepting the rider, you receive a minimum guaranteed rate of return. But what difference does a guaranteed rate of return make, if you'll never have access to your money again? Obviously, I am not a fan of these tools, even though for many years I have been licensed to sell them.

There is a federal law guaranteeing that the owner of one of these tools will receive all their money back, if they realize within three years that they did not fully understand everything about the product they bought. This is not surprising, since ninety percent of the people licensed to sell these products don't fully understand them either. There is a whole lot of money to be made in commissions and fees by selling variable annuities, and that's enough incentive for some salespeople.

WHAT'S IN IT FOR ME?

We receive calls and e-mails every day from people all over the world who are fearful of an impending economic collapse. Without a doubt, the majority of these callers want to know where to buy gold, and how much they should have on hand when the economy finally plummets to its eventual demise. Callers from the United States are most worried about the death of the dollar, because they heard on some television show or a radio or internet program that the U.S. currency will die by a certain date.

Some call in because they combine fear-filled stories they hear on these shows with Biblical prophecy. The big fears of these callers revolve around the idea that in the "last days" of the world there will be only one worldwide currency. In other words, that every country on earth will use the exact same currency, so we will all have to use the same currency if we wish to buy or sell anything, from food to cleaning supplies.

Now I'm not a Biblical scholar, but I have read the Bible several times and I have researched many sermons that I've preached and classes I've taught. The particular scripture these people refer to can be found in Revelation 13:17, which talks about how people will buy and sell goods in the end times. The truth is that this scripture describes a system that will be used to conduct business; it is **not** describing a single currency.

I can't think of any single message relating to this idea that doesn't also promote the idea that everyone should go out and buy gold or silver. Some of the most panicked calls come from people who have heard a particular pastor speak on the importance of buying gold or silver, saying that will be the only way people will be able to transact business.

I was once invited to speak at such a pastor's church to discuss end-times prophecy and the current economic situation. The inviting pastor had seen me on television with another pastor, who focuses on the death of the US dollar and various other conspiracy theories. The inviting pastor therefore thought that I would tell everyone that there is no safety in traditional investments and that our banks were teetering on the brink of complete collapse.

After we completed the two-day conference, the pastor seemed angry with me. I asked him why he seemed less than pleased with my message. I had no idea that this pastor, only the week before, had sealed a deal with a gold broker to sell precious metals on commission, to supplement his income from the church. This pastor had his church pay my speaking fee and expenses to travel halfway across the country to deliver a message which he was sure would enable him to profit personally.

I know you've heard fantastic speakers like Rush Limbaugh, Sean Hannity, Glenn Beck, and Alex Jones tell us how important it is to protect ourselves by purchasing gold and other precious metals for our portfolio. Entertainers like these get paid millions of dollars each year to promote their sponsors. Most of these entertainers benefit from you buying gold and other precious metals. This is exactly why I do not accept any advertising for our radio show or other media outlets with which we may be blessed.

You can rest assured that all teachings from the Financial Leadership Academy, all messages that I deliver, and all classes we sponsor will always focus on the truth. We are committed to providing you with reliable and unbiased messages, and we will never compromise that message simply because it is not what someone else wants us to say.

No matter what story you hear or what report someone tells you about, you must ask the source of the information this crucial question: "What's in it for you?"

UNDERSTANDING LIFE INSURANCE

BECAUSE LIFE INSURANCE IS PROBABLY the most debated, misunderstood, and convoluted financial tool in existence, I felt it deserved a section all to itself so we could uncover its true benefits and limitations.

We've all heard famous entertainers on the radio and television telling us that we should all by term life insurance and invest in mutual funds. These entertainers go so far as to promise us that we'll see an average of 12% return from our mutual funds each year.

Friends, that single claim should cause you to tune your radio to a different station and never listen to that person about financial matters ever again. It is against the law for licensed financial professionals to make such absurd claims.

We could be locked up in jail, and would certainly lose our license for making such outrageous projections. I actually called the federal agency that oversees the financial industry, FINRA, to ask about these people. I wanted to know how they could get by with making these ridiculous statements that will end up harming others.

I was told that since they are not licensed, they aren't subject to the laws that pertain to professionals in our field. I was told that non-licensed people may give each other all the advice in the world, without regard for ramifications. The person I spoke with said that people just need to be smart enough to listen to licensed professionals.

That told me a lot about our industry, and the effectiveness of aggressive marketing campaigns. For example, we hear advertisements in the media and on the internet dozens of times each day about how inexpensive it is to buy term life insurance.

What these advertisements don't tell us is that only about 1% (yes, one percent) of term life insurance policies ever actually pay out a death benefit. That means almost all premiums paid to life insurance companies for term life insurance are pure profit for the companies.

Since I'm not trying to sell you any product, and I don't even know what your needs are, please allow me to share some unbiased information that will aid you when sorting through all the hype to determine exactly what's right for you.

Permanent life insurance is not an investment, because it provides you with guaranteed returns: think of it as a supercharged saving account.

I don't believe there is one perfect life insurance policy that covers your every need. Plain and simple, if anyone tries to tell you that all you need is a permanent policy or a term policy, they have no idea what they're doing, and you should politely walk away from them and seek competent guidance. The same is true for those who tell you that if you just invest wisely now, then someday you'll be able to "self-insure", and you won't need any life insurance at all.

The truth of the matter is, the different types of life insurance were designed to effectively accomplish specific jobs, just as automobiles were designed for and are best suited for specific jobs. Would you use a Corvette to haul a pallet of concrete blocks to a job site? Would you use an old farm tractor as your primary mode of transportation to take a cross country trip with your family? Would you select a big recreation vehicle to race with high-performance cars?

I know these examples are all ridiculous, but the thought that any one type of life insurance product can perform every desired function is just as absurd. And the thought that you don't need any life insurance at all is absolutely ludicrous.

To better understand why I make these statements let's first take a look at what any type of insurance does. What I'm about to share with you pertains to every type of insurance, whether it's the insurance you have to protect your cell phone, your homeowners insurance, or your health or auto insurance.

Insurance, by its very nature, is designed to share risk. If you have homeowners insurance and a storm destroys your roof, you pay a deductible, and then the insurance company accepts the remainder of the risk. This is the same philosophy behind your auto insurance, cell phone, or appliance warranty, as well as your health and life insurance. The risk is shared between the insured (you) and the insurer (the insurance company).

Is there any larger risk that needs to be covered than your very existence, and your ability to provide for your family? To say that there will be a day when you will no longer need life insurance, as these entertainers do, requires us to ask ourselves if the day will ever come when we will no longer need homeowners, health, or auto insurance.

The only major difference between life insurance and these other types of coverage is variations in the coverage.

All the other types of coverage we discussed are actually term life insurance. With your cell phone insurance, for example, the insurance company accepts a portion of the risk beyond your deductible as long as you pay your premium. After your premium payments stop, the company has no obligation to assume the risk that you might drop your phone in a lake.

So if you drop your phone in water the day after your coverage ends, you are on your own, and you assume all the risk. All the money you paid the insurance company is now profit for them, with no benefit to you. Understanding this simple example will help you realize the true benefit of term life insurance.

Term life insurance is perfect for sharing risk on temporary needs such as short-term loans or temporary financial obligations. Think of term life insurance the same way you would temporary housing: you would probably rent a house only until you decided on a permanent residence. Once you determine where your permanent home will be, you would naturally decide to buy it, right?

Your decision to purchase a home instead of continuing to rent is more than likely because you want to build some equity in your future. With the value of your property increasing, you have an opportunity to access that equity to use it for other purposes.

Let's apply this same principle of ownership to your life insurance policy. Since we now realize that the entire reason for owning insurance is to share risk of loss, why would we ever want to be without coverage?

I started this discussion by mentioning some famous people who earn their living by promoting their advertisers and selling the products they're paid to endorse. It is therefore appropriate to share some real life examples of how some other very famous people, who had competent guidance, implemented permanent life insurance to change the world.

In my last book, *The Love of Money: How to Build Wealth and Not Be Corrupted*, I told how **Walt Disney** used the equity in his life insurance policy as start-up money for what is now the Disney business empire.

Mr. Disney borrowed from himself (from his whole-life insurance policy) and mortgaged his home, because no bank would fund his dream. In essence, Mr. Disney became his own bank—simply by using permanent life insurance exactly as it was designed.

Ray Kroc was the founder of the McDonalds corporation. We all know McDonalds to be arguably the most successful food distribution business in the world today. Mr. Kroc used his permanent life insurance policy as his personal bank in the early years as his business grew. Mr.Kroc did not take a salary from his new venture for the first eight years. Instead, he borrowed from his permanent life insurance policy to pay himself and key employees.

Having access to your own money, without having to borrow it from a bank, is always a good idea. Having access to tax-free money makes that good idea an idea of genius. *(Remember: Always seek the guidance of a tax professional in areas relating to your personal tax liability.)*

Doris Christopher, a stay-at-home mom with two daughters, started her business while searching for a new career. Using $3,000 she borrowed from a permanent life insurance policy, Christopher bought some basic inventory: kitchen shears, spatulas, other basics, and some lumber for crates to hold her products. Her $3,000 seed money grew into a multi-level marketing business—that Warren Buffet bought in 2002 for $1.5 billion. The little business she built using her life insurance policy is what you and I know as Pampered Chef.

James Cash Penney, the son of a poor Baptist preacher, had a vision for selling dry goods through retail stores. Penney began with only one store in a small Wyoming town, yet his dream grew to be valued at over $14 billion. The retail company that bears his name, J.C. Penney, is now a nationwide American business empire.

But Penney's dream was nearly wiped out in 1929 when the stock market crashed. He rebounded with money he borrowed from his permanent life insurance policy. That necessary access to cash kept him in business.

Penney's $3 million whole-life insurance policy was there for him not only in death, but also in life. That's how you need to view permanent life insurance: not as a bill you have to pay, but as a combination savings account and life protection policy.

I'll share one more story with you about how helpful permanent life insurance can be. This story is not about some famous person with a huge business empire or millions of dollars in life insurance. I want to tell you about one of my own family members. I can't give you his real name, but just know that he is a very close relation to me. For the purposes of this story we'll just call him Jerry.

Jerry and I were visiting at his home, talking on his back deck as he was grilling some hamburgers for dinner. He was telling me how he and his wife really needed to expand their home. Their kids were getting older, and the small home they had built nearly 20 years earlier was now cramped.

As we discussed the expansion plans, Jerry shared with me the one stumbling block that prevented them from moving forward: how to fund such a project on his salary. I offered to connect Jerry with a mortgage specialist who was part of my professional network, to see if Jerry could qualify for a loan.

Jerry started getting quotes from contractors, and before long he called me to say they had a plan together. Jerry's biggest concern now was that they were so close to paying off their current mortgage. Did they really want to go back into debt for a new 30-year mortgage? He asked me to review his financial picture and make some recommendations.

I found some areas where Jerry could use some of the borrowed money and pay off other debt, thereby reducing his monthly obligation to debtors by $1,800 per month. His new mortgage was going to cost about $200 per month more than the original. With this $1,600 net increase in his monthly income, I recommended that Jerry start a permanent life insurance policy.

We then compared the amortization schedule from the mortgage company with the guaranteed returns of his whole-life insurance policy. When I ran the illustration, Jerry and I were both amazed to see that—in just 11 years—the cash value in his policy would be enough to pay off his new mortgage completely. Since his old mortgage only had 10 years left, Jerry was exuberant: he would be able to double the size of his home, pay off all his other debt, and only add one more year to the life of his mortgage—simply by using permanent life insurance properly. (We filled the remainder of his insurance need with a 15-year term insurance policy.)

I can tell you countless stories of people, whom I've personally helped, who have achieved their dreams by using life insurance. One thing all these people have in common, though, is that I didn't simply sell them term or permanent insurance: I used both types, to make sure that all their insurance needs were covered.

Friends, please don't allow famous people on the radio or television to sway your judgment. Don't allow them to sell you what their advertisers pay them millions of dollars to market to you.

Don't allow them to convince you that one day you won't need life insurance because your mutual funds will have created so much wealth that you can be "self-insured."

You probably pay for (life) insurance on your cell phone, in case you drop it in the toilet. Isn't your life as important as your cell phone? At what point do you think you'll be able to self-insure your home, and so no longer need to pay for homeowners insurance?

At what point will you be able to self-insure your automobiles, or no longer feel the need to purchase an extended warranty on that new computer or toaster oven? Let's take a rational look at financial matters, and stop looking at them emotionally.

Life insurance is a wonderful tool when used properly. A good combination of the proper amount and type of coverage can provide you with accessibility to cash while you're alive, plus the funds to protect your family or business in the case of death.

(Remember, always seek guidance from a CFLA (Certified Financial Leadership Advisor) to help you plan a strategy that's right for you. They understand what I've shared with you, and they know the importance of using the right tool for the right job at the right time. Find out more about life insurance and other financial tools at www.myifla.com.)

NOW THAT I HAVE THIS KNOWLEDGE, WHAT SHOULD I DO WITH IT?

NOW THAT YOU FULLY UNDERSTAND that you are being taken advantage of by many banks and investment companies, you should be motivated to make some changes in how you view and use your money.

It's been said that a man can change the entire world by simply changing the way he looks at it. If enough of us change the way we use our money, we can actually change the entire economic future of our country—and eventually the world.

Just as for a drug addict or someone in an abusive relationship, the first step to freedom is recognizing that you have a problem. You've taken that first step already, simply by reading this book.

The next thing you should do is join with like-minded people at www.myifla.com, to stay informed of developments and ways you can better position yourself to recognize and implement effective proactive financial strategies. Once you join our peaceful revolution, you can draw from articles, specially-designed classes, and gatherings that will offer you even more information and encouragement.

After you begin implementing these principles in your own life, you will naturally want to share them with others. When you're ready to become a leader and to offer hope and guidance to others, those resources are also available to you through the Financial Leadership Academy. As we develop leaders in each community, we will grow a grassroots movement of people who are empowered, and who want to make a difference.

When any group of people are passionate about their mission and have the understanding and the leadership to take effective action, they become an unstoppable force.

The unstoppable force we are building through this peaceful revolution will not only give us control over our economic system, but will give us the ability to take back our governmental system as well. I envision a combined movement—made up of the Tea Party, the Fair Tax Initiative, and the Christian community—that will stand up and be recognized as one huge voting block.

When that many people who are passionate about the same issues come together as one to voice and vote their beliefs, changes occur. This is what happened in 2008, and it led to the election of President Barack Hussein Obama in the United States; several groups banded together in an effort to completely derail the values and foundation of our great nation.

It is the responsibility of every citizen to take action for what they believe. Anyone unwilling to sacrifice to ensure the rights of all of us doesn't deserve the rights to begin with.

Here's what you need to do:

1. Join the economic revolution (International Financial Leadership Association).
2. Become trained in Financial Leadership, by attending one of our live training events.
3. Practice Financial Leadership in your life.
4. Take the no-cost, 21-day "Become a Millionaire Challenge" at www.myifla.com.
5. Share what you've learned with others (for example, encourage your pastor to attend a CFLC class).
6. Elect political leaders who reflect your beliefs.
7. Make sure we never become financial slaves again!

Here is a simple, practical, but powerful first step to help you begin to take control of your money. Below is a sample of the financial tracking form we use at the Academy to show you who is actually benefiting from each of your hard-earned dollars, so you can identify the areas of your finances that you need to regain control over.

(Once you join the Financial Leadership revolution you can access an interactive version of this form at our website, www.myifla.com. You will then be able to input your personal numbers and have the computer automatically calculate the data for you. Or you could make a paper copy of this form, replacing the sample data with your actual numbers.)

Family Budget Tracking Chart

	Total Projected Cost	Total Actual Cost	Total Difference
	$1,195	$1,236	($41)

Projected Monthly Income	
Income 1	$4,000
Income 2	$1,300
Extra income	$300
Total monthly income	$5,600

Actual Monthly Income	
Income 1	$4,000
Income 2	$1,300
Extra income	$300
Total monthly income	$5,600

Projected balance (Projected income minus expenses)	$4,405
Actual balance (Actual income minus expenses)	$4,364
Difference (Actual minus projected)	($41)

Housing

	Projected Cost	Actual Cost	Difference
Mortgage or rent	$1,000	$1,000	$0
Second mortgage or rent	$0	$0	$0
Phone	$54	$100	($46)
Electricity	$44	$56	($12)
Gas	$22	$28	($6)
Water and sewer	$8	$8	$0
Cable	$34	$34	$0
Waste removal	$10	$10	$0
Maintenance or repairs	$23	$0	$23
Supplies	$0	$0	$0
Other	$0	$0	$0
Subtotals	$1,195	$1,236	($41)

Transportation

Vehicle 1 payment			$0
Vehicle 2 payment			$0
Bus/taxi fare			$0
Insurance			$0
Licensing			$0
Fuel			$0
Maintenance			$0
Other			$0
Subtotals	$0	$0	$0

Insurance

Home			$0
Health			$0
Life			$0
Other			$0
Subtotals	$0	$0	$0

Food

Groceries			$0
Dining out			$0
Other			$0
Subtotals	$0	$0	$0

Children

Medical			$0
Clothing			$0
School tuition			$0
School supplies			$0
Organization dues or fees			$0
Lunch money			$0
Child care			$0
Toys/games			$0
Other			$0
Subtotals	$0	$0	$0

Pets

Food			$0
Medical			$0
Grooming			$0
Toys			$0
Other			$0
Subtotals	$0	$0	$0

Personal Care

Medical			$0
Hair/nails			$0
Clothing			$0
Dry cleaning			$0
Health club			$0
Organization dues or fees			$0
Other			$0
Subtotals	$0	$0	$0

Entertainment

	Projected Cost	Actual Cost	Difference
Video/DVD			$0
CDs			$0
Movies			$0
Concerts			$0
Sporting events			$0
Live theater			$0
Other			$0
Subtotals	$0	$0	$0

Loans

Personal			$0
Student			$0
Credit card			$0
Credit card			$0
Credit card			$0
Other			$0
Subtotals	$0	$0	$0

Taxes

Federal			$0
State			$0
Local			$0
Other			$0
Subtotals	$0	$0	$0

Savings or Investments

Retirement account			$0
Investment account			$0
College			$0
Other			$0
Subtotals	$0	$0	$0

Gifts and Donations

Charity 1			$0
Charity 2			$0
Charity 3			$0
Subtotals	$0	$0	$0

Legal

Attorney			$0
Alimony			$0
Payments on lien or judgment			$0
Other			$0
Subtotals	$0	$0	$0

IN CONCLUSION

It is my sincere prayer that the words in this book have given you a better understanding of what has occurred in our nation's financial services market, and how it has impacted you and why.

I also pray that God will reveal to you the best way you can use this knowledge to benefit you and your family, and bring glory to Him.

If you need personal guidance or are not sure you can do this on your own, we have trained and experienced professionals who are willing and ready to serve you. We also have an army of people who are happy to share their experiences and offer you guidance and encouragement.

If you would like to become a leader in our financial revolution, just let us know at the Financial Leadership Academy. We will let you know when the next CFLC (Certified Financial Leadership Counselor) class will be, and where you can attend one of these classes near you.

As you move forward with taking back control of your money, you need to stay strong. Nothing worth having has ever been easy. You worked hard to earn your money, now you'll have to work to be able to keep it. If we all work together, and not for any particular political party, we can take our lives back!

Action: Individuals take back control of their money. **Reaction:** The people collectively take back control of their government and a prosperous way of life!

INDEX

For more information about
Rodney D. Ballance
&

THE 7 INDISPUTABLE LAWS OF
FINANCIAL LEADERSHIP
please visit:

www.rodneyballance.com
www.facebook.com/financialleadershipacademy
@RodneyBallance

....

For more information about
AMBASSADOR INTERNATIONAL
please visit:

www.ambassador-international.com
@AmbassadorIntl
www.facebook.com/AmbassadorIntl

9 961 41521CB00011B/2423 I2072173471

www.ingramcontent.com/pod-product-compliance
Lightning Source LLC
Chambersburg PA
CBHW050512210326
41521CB00011B/2423